INSPIRE ACTION

TABLE OF CONTENTS

PREFACE

Introductions from Industry Weapon Executive Team 9

Acknowledgements 18

CHAPTER 1: THE PSYCHOLOGY OF VISUAL COMMUNICATION   23

Digital Signage is Reigning Supreme in Marketing 25

How Multimedia Meets Multitasking 26

Vulnerability is a Valuable Asset 28

A Few Thoughts on the Subconscious Mind 31

Fun + Habits + Impact = Trust 33

CHAPTER 2: MASTERING THE AUDIENCE ENGAGEMENT FRAMEWORK   37

3 Keys to Battling Digital Irrelevance 39

Designing Visuals for Engagement: Motion, Visuals, Time
and Color 40

The Data Content Ratio 44

Quick Tips: Effectively Incorporating Instagram into Your Design 47

The Purpose of Devices 48

Bringing Digital Purpose into Healthcare 50

Case Study: AngioDynamics 53

* Trial and Error of Manufacturing Productivity Tools

* Real-Time Data Visuals Revolutionize the Production Floor

* Building Morale in an Organic Way

CHAPTER 3: THE FOUR QUADRANTS OF VISUAL ENGAGEMENT   61

Motion: The Movement of Media 63

Motion in Action 64

Visuals: So Vital, and So Easily Done Wrong 65

Graphic Design Basics 65

Time: Disinterest is Nothing to be Apathetic About 67

Color: Casting the Emotional Tone 69

Case Study: College of the Canyons 72

* Additional Analysis

Chapter 4: Understanding Visual Storytelling 77
The Three Tickets to Employee Retention 77

* Publicize

* Promote

* Project Vision

Getting a Grasp on Company Culture 81

How Company Culture Impacts the Bottom Line 83

A Closer Look: Retention in Law Firms 84

Case Studies: Highwoods Properties and Orvis 86

  ✦ It Worked? Time to Up the Ante

  ✦ Socially Relevant Stories

  ✦ Authenticity is Everything

  ✦ Creating Personalized Experiences

CHAPTER 5: TALKING TECH—UNDERSTANDING PURPOSE, LIMITATIONS, AND AVAILABILITY   95

What is a Purpose-Based Device? 96

The Differences Between Interactivity and Visual-Only 97

Know Your Limitations Before Running Full-Speed Ahead. 98

A Closer Look: How Digital Integrations Flopped in Fast-Food 102

Case Study: Quicken Loans Arena 104

CHAPTER 6: WHAT DO WE DO WITH ATTENTION ONCE WE HAVE IT?   107

Seeing Social Relevance in Action 109

Making the Most of Corporate Communications 109

Code Red: A Few Notes on Emergency Messaging 111

Acquaint Yourself with These Acronyms: KPIs, SLA and SELs 112

Using Data to Boost Sales Without Becoming Big Brother 115

How Data and Social Integrations can Impact Business ... 116

A Favorite Internet Strategy is to Use our VOICE 117

How One of Our Clients is Fighting the Battle with Digital Signage 125

Digital Signage in the K-12 Space 126

    • It's Long Past Time to Make Safety a Priority

    • Using Tech to Stimulate Apathetic Students

    • Change is Good, Kid

Influencers are Having a Moment… 133

...But Use Them Wisely 134

Closing Thoughts 136

Endnotes 138

Digital Signage Buyers Guide 139

Notes 151

PREFACE

FROM WIL CHUFO, BUSINESS PARTNER & CTO AT INDUSTRY WEAPON:

My first recommendation for Dave was written in February 2007, in which I called him an "excellent facilitator" who champions "groundbreaking products and business models." That's still accurate, but it only scratches the surface.

In the years since I wrote that rec, Dave has honed these skills with an uncanny ability to listen and learn. His dedication to understanding the ever-changing landscape with continued education, combining his existing expertise with new knowledge, consistently enables him to lead and succeed. Dave's portfolio of experiences and solutions are key to defining challenges and presenting these time tested solutions. This book is a testament to years of program and process development that have helped influence, and continue to shape, the future of communication in digital media.

Within months of writing that first recommendation, we had formed the partnership that would become Industry Weapon; another year later, we'd begin developing CommandCenterHD, the innovative platform that powers digital signage across the globe. So much has been accomplished and learned over the past 10-plus years, and there's a whole lot more from Dave in the years to come.

FROM CRAIG HANNA, BUSINESS PARTNER & COO:

Dave, Wil and I were introduced to each other through a mutual friend in 2006 who knew we'd all click. There were key similarities between the businesses we were separately running, and our long-term goals were uniquely aligned. A partnership just felt obvious to pursue.

At first, we passed projects back and forth between our companies— Wil and I had a ton of technology that Dave could utilize for his customers, while Dave had a huge network of contacts that Wil and I could leverage to generate business. But we quickly realized that the three of us were much stronger together than we were apart, so after a year of casual collaboration, we decided to merge our companies on Saint Patrick's Day in 2007. We joke that we're like the old Reese's commercial: "Hey, you got peanut butter in my chocolate / You got chocolate in my peanut butter." We were simply meant to work together.

Fast forward another year, and by dumb luck, we were presented with an opportunity in February of 2008 by one of the largest tech companies in the world to get involved with their digital signage practice by leveraging the technologies we'd created for e-commerce and web sites. Their customers were unhappy with the content management system they had created, which was being sold with the digital signage hardware. It wasn't working. Could we provide the solution?

We weren't sure. We didn't even know what digital signage was at the time. But we had faith in each other, and in our team, to evolve our business model and focus 100 percent on digital signage.

In hindsight it was the right call, but early on, it looked like a bad bet. In order to make the switch, we had to hit the pause button on looking for new e-commerce and website projects. That meant we had to invest any money we made back into the business. The only feasible route was for Dave, Wil and I to work without a single paycheck for as long as possible. And no, this wasn't three young, single guys living on the edge — we all had new babies (either born or on the way) and wives who'd quit their jobs because we had, up until this point, established career stability. The timing was terrible. But we saw the opportunity at hand and knew that this might be the only real chance to grab it.

At the same time that we were refocusing our efforts on digital signage, we also began looking for investors to help us create a little bit of leeway to continue to operate. For months, everyone we met with said no. It felt like we had exhausted the entire local investment community. We weren't asking for much.

On May 14th, 2008 I had $0 in the bank, Wil — whose wife was on maternity leave from teaching — had $1,000, and Dave was newly without a house. He'd been forced to sell it earlier that month. Through all of that turmoil, we kept our promise of keeping our employees paid. They never missed a check.

It was heartbreaking and stressful. After a Hail Mary, last-ditch effort phone call didn't bring home the bacon, we bumped into an investment duo totally by chance. They liked what we had to say, they liked what they saw with our technology, and our makeshift tents and sleeping bags in the office reminded them of when they got their start. That day was May 15th, 2008.

So, on May 15th, 2008 we got a little bit of cash, we retained majority ownership in the company, and were now off to the races to attack the digital signage industry.

There are so many small but meaningful victories I could include, but suffice it to say that within a few months we started landing customers, and within two years we became profitable and debt free...which we have maintained to this day! Along the way, we've been met with serious challenges that have tested our abilities and our relationships, but our faith and respect for each other is what keeps us glued together and moving forward.

We each remember exactly what it feels like to be broke, to not be able to pay bills, to wonder if you're going to have a house to live in tomorrow, to wonder what you are going to tell your wife and your children when you have no money. We don't ever want to go back to that feeling, and we don't want other entrepreneurs to endure it, either. To this day, our motivation is fueled by staying humble yet aggressive and by keeping each other honest with who we are and what our company stands for.

FROM JORDAN TSVETKOFF, BUSINESS PARTNER & DIRECTOR OF ARCHITECTURE

Dave took on the task of building an industry-leading digital signage company from the ground up over the course of the last 10 years. His combination of innovative selling techniques and a no-holds-barred quest for new markets led to exponential growth of the company's client base. Devotion to not only business metrics but also personal goals personifies his non-stop desire to promote an attitude of success and winning.

FROM BRIAN PULLMAN, DIRECTOR OF SUPPORT & ONBOARDING

I've known Dave since I was sixteen years old -- met him at Friendly's skating in the parking lot. From being kids up through present day, I've gravitated toward Dave in large part because he is a phenomenal communicator. When you talk to Dave, he's more involved in your side of the conversation than his. He's genuinely interested in what each and every person has to say. For me, that's one of the biggest reasons why I qualify him as an expert in communications. He listens and reacts and learns.

I've been fortunate to work with and for Dave at several companies. As soon as he starts working on something (or even starts thinking about working on something), he instinctively decides to become an expert on that subject. An example: We used to work in the business of garment decoration and distribution for professional sports. Not only did Dave make use of his deep knowledge of manufacturing, but he also became an expert in the actual equipment used from start to finish of the process. When we got into that industry, the standard turnaround time for ordering a custom jersey and seeing it arrive at your door was six to eight weeks. Dave's relentless determination to research and develop the best possible system cut that into an unbelievable 10-day turnaround.

I'd be remiss if I didn't also note how Dave treats his employees. In the past, I've worked with and for people who just were not ethical. They didn't care to understand or connect with their employees; they'd tell their people one thing and act a totally different way. Industry Weapon is built on the foundation of treating people right. People work hard for Dave, and they want to, because he gets down in the trenches with them and truly rewards them for their efforts.

Industry Weapon utilizes some of the foremost technology in the world, but Dave doesn't see things that way. He doesn't focus on that. It's not about how cool the tech is (and it is cool), it's about how it can be used to improve communication in the world. He really views digital signage as a means to impact lives.

FROM CHRISTIAN ARMSTRONG, BUSINESS PARTNER & DIRECTOR OF MARKETING

When I first met Dave, I was a 25-year-old graphic designer with a small freelance design business. Dave's business was primarily focused on consulting in professional sports licensing, sales and business development. My day job was at a fashion retailer that was looking to sell its unique product line to pro sports teams, but it was struggling to make the right connections. That kind of challenge was right up Dave's alley when he signed on as a consultant.

The spring of 2006 was a complete blur as this so-called "consultant" took a company that was struggling to get an order from the local NFL team and transformed it overnight into a company fulfilling millions in orders from **every** team in the NFL. The entrepreneurial drive, business acumen, and passion that he possessed was on a completely different level from anything I'd seen before. This guy was a tireless networker with a Rolodex that seemed to never end.

We started working on some collaborations, and as he combined his business with Craig and Wil's, my freelance business was absorbed into the newly-born Industry Weapon.

Dave's networking skills have enabled him to create supposed once-in-a-lifetime opportunities over and over again. He has the ability to communicate with people in a very relatable way, engaging people of all walks of life with real, meaningful and impactful conversation.

He always cares more about the person he is speaking with than he does about promoting himself. He asks questions — tons of questions — and, through this curiosity, he develops a deep understanding about each person or organization's specific challenge. This innate ability has repeatedly proven invaluable in business and in life.

A perfect example of this is the turning point of our organization. Years ago, a wild misadventure put Dave in a car with a total stranger for 8 hours. 24 hours later, CommandCenterHD was born and the company's focus was quickly redirected toward this emerging technology — that, at the time, we knew absolutely nothing about. But we trusted Dave, and we trusted the strange turn of events that brought this software to Industry Weapon.

In those days, we worked through the weekend. Dave once called me at 9AM on a Sunday morning and said, "Let's crank out an interface for the digital signage project." I headed straight to his house and we dove into designing the interface right then and there. After several hours, we had the initial wireframes for what would become CommandCenterHD.

I'm not sure that he knows that I unintentionally overheard this, but while we were working that Sunday, Dave took a call from the other room. The quiet conversation was Dave apologizing to his wife, who was trying to buy groceries, for maxing out the credit card. I had not realized, until that point, the incredible risks that he, Craig, and Wil were taking to get this company off the ground.

Ensuring that employees were paid first was a substantial burden, and it took an unimaginable amount of determination and bravery to lead the company through those tough beginnings. Dave's leadership and poise was unwavering during this critical time in the company's young history. His focus and determination allowed our team to rapidly and effectively learn the mechanics of how to go to market in an industry none of us had any real experience in.

Dave has a remarkable ability to take complex problems and easily identify their key components, enabling us to adapt and build a new strategy to keep progressing forward. He is quick to learn everything about a given topic and almost overnight become an established expert. He seeks knowledge and upon finding the crux of the specific problem he creates his solution.

From there, he pitches it, he promotes it and he refines it again and again, inspiring those around him to participate in growing the idea. It's through this process that our business has continued to flourish year over year.

When it comes to handling customers, I've watched Dave make decisions that I'd imagine most CEOs in companies of any size would balk at. Like replacing hundreds of thousands of dollars of equipment for a customer free of charge when a manufacturer error rendered that client's equipment useless.

This was the ethically responsible decision, a decision squarely focused on doing right by the customer and not on the bottom line. I've seen this unorthodox decision-making process repeated time and time again—and it always brought me back to that first phone call, when he and the other founders of Industry Weapon put their livelihoods on the line for the good of their employees and a company they believed in.

For the past 12 years, Dave has been a source of inspiration and encouragement to the people he leads. Always looking to grow and improve himself, he's never satisfied with the status quo. His creativity and vision have created solutions that have helped some of the biggest brands in the world solve their communications problems. That's why we're so excited to bring you his story, in his own words, and the lessons we've learned (so far!) with Industry Weapon.

ACKNOWLEDGEMENTS

I have had a passion to create for as long as I can remember. I credit my mom and dad for giving me the confidence to be bullish with my thoughts and ideas of what is possible. From a very early age, I was encouraged to practice, experiment, and when necessary, fail with a curiosity to continue to pursue my goals.

My wife DaniElle, who has boundless amounts of energy and always gets behind my ideas—and when necessary, gives me a swift kick in the butt when I need to execute those ideas without hesitation.

My kids, Ava, Will, and Grey, who taught me a much bigger "why" about living.

The four guys, Craig, Wil, Christian and Jordan, who risked their careers to make sure that these ideas were successful.

Eric and Mike, who could have invested in tons of other companies with much more impressive business models, but they chose Industry Weapon and supported the business with confidence, giving us the security to grow this business well beyond our imagination.

I am humbled and grateful for the people who have and continue to show up in my life. The amazing personalities who help build on ideas and motivate me to go after bigger goals with a fierce persistence.

And who could have imagined, it all started with a dog bite. :)

DaniElle, David, Ava, Will and Grey

Dave's Parents John and Elaine Wible

Jordan, Craig, Wil, Christian & Dave

THE AUDIENCE ENGAGEMENT FRAMEWORK™

A clearly defined structure which makes up today's most successful digital communications deployments

*Content examples for demonstration only. Real categories can vary.

CHAPTER 1

THE PSYCHOLOGY OF VISUAL COMMUNICATION

The Canadian philosopher Marshall McLuhan famously said, "The medium is the message." He passed away decades before advanced digital tech would become part of our world, but his point proves true as ever when we talk about how to effectively utilize video walls and digital signage.

Before our clients come to really understand how to leverage this technology, I repeatedly hear variations of the same core mistake: They treat their digital signage like it's any other TV or laptop. "It's great!" one CEO told me of his new video wall. "I can just throw our website up on the big screen, and we're off to the races!"

Nope! Not quite. In fact, that's a really good way to make sure nobody notices your signage at all.

Here's what often happens with brand-new clients who approach Industry Weapon looking for guidance: They have video walls already in place, which they've been using as a large monitor for media designed for laptops or smartphones. Instead of treating the video wall of its own separate medium, they've assigned it a super basic task — even though it's capable of so much more.

These new clients are genuinely baffled that few people are pausing for even a moment to consume the content on-screen.

Consider, for a moment, what type of content *is* going up on those company video walls. More often than not, bland company memos (often accompanied by clip-art; guys, this isn't 2006!), audio-muted YouTube videos and dated B-roll footage scroll by on a loop. Aesthetically, it's not much different from a screensaver that appears on your computer screen when you've been idle for too long. We've long been trained to ignore those screens, and we do the exact same thing with unstimulating video walls.

If you've been to New York's Times Square anytime in the past decade, you know exactly what I'm talking about. Imagine wandering onto 42nd Street just to be blinded by screen after screen of black text on static marquees. Who would bother taking a touristy picture of that? You might as well be comparing screens in a Best Buy.

Dynamic digital signage has its own entire category of strengths. Today more than ever, these screens aren't meant to function like glowing billboards. But because digital signage is a relatively new and niche medium, few people really understand the incredible depths to which they can be optimized — or how to put those features into action. When the guys and I got to work on Industry Weapon, we were some of the first in the world to grasp just how powerful digital signage can be. When done correctly, it improves employee retention, boosts morale, reduces personnel costs and bumps productivity up a notch.

We've created a thriving business introducing digital signage into all types of industries across the world. I'm excited to walk you through just how we did it, and how we continue to do it.

DIGITAL SIGNAGE IS REIGNING SUPREME IN MARKETING

The CEO I mentioned before — the one who tossed his company website up on a video wall and called it a day — soon came to understand that he was missing a huge opportunity. Let me first say, I *really* do understand where his fundamental mistake was coming from. After all, at face value, the digital sign can definitely look like your everyday big TV or computer monitor. So I can see why so many people are quick to broadcast the same information they'd usually watch via those mediums.

That being said, his first strategy for content was totally misguided.

What we at Industry Weapon have discovered — through a whole lot of testing and case studies and real-world installations — is that people don't interact with a digital sign or video wall the same way that they interact with their personal computers or iPhones. It's a new animal. And, when you think about it, that makes a lot of sense.

When I open my laptop or unlock my phone, I do it for a reason: To answer a text, to order my kid a gift, to stream Joe Rogan's podcast on YouTube. I have a specific task (even if that task is as simple as "I want to mindlessly scroll through Facebook until someone's vacation photos catch my attention").

The difference with a video wall? It's a big, shared device, not a personal one. Nobody passing by feels that pressing individual need to take a look. At first, that may seem like a negative, but it's actually not. While personal devices are used electively, the digital sign is there whether you're looking for it or not — which means that, while our brains automatically have a different reaction than they do to a phone, we can channel that reaction in a meaningful way.

Compared to phones and computers, where time of engagement may be minutes or even hours, people naturally engage with digital signage peripherally. They'll notice it for just a glance — unless the content really captivates them, and there's an art to that. It's not as simple (or gaudy) as showcasing loud colors or brash, shocking messaging. Thankfully, as a society, we're long past that! We all know what clickbait looks like and how fruitless the end content always is, and the same principle applies to digital signage: If it looks untrustworthy or somehow misleading, we look away.

This presents an interesting challenge: How can you grab people's attention quickly and keep their engagement, without sacrificing quality of content? Answer: The signage must be truly eye-catching and relevant-feeling. Most importantly, it must be specifically optimized for the platform.

What captivates a person on Instagram is not equivalent to what'll appeal to them on a video wall. In some ways, the anti-quated-feeling billboard alongside the highway still manages to get this right. A really good, well-crafted billboard ad actually works. (That's why they're still around, and why brands spend big bucks to rent them!) In practice, this means two things: Remain visual-first, meaning prioritize optics over all else. And two, try to minimize the amount of information so it's digestible.

HOW MULTIMEDIA MEETS MULTITASKING

Advertising minds already know this, but the human brain can only parse so much information at a glance. The goal is to convey enough in that single glance that it keeps the eye glued for the appropriate amount of time.

Not everyone multitasks while they're on their phones, but certainly our smartphones have increased our desire for instant gratification. How many times have you closed out an app because cell service sucks and was taking too long to load? We expect to receive and process information very quickly. Your digital signage message should be designed to deliver that short burst of visual information. It can also, when necessary, feature number-heavy analysis. But even then, there are ways to deploy that data, concisely.

Consider how some clients are initially resistant to the idea of "white space," but any designer — digital or otherwise — will tell you just how important these clean, neutral areas are. Clutter isn't appealing. It may feel unavoidable, especially when you're dealing with numbers (I've had some clients come to me with programming that looked like an Excel spreadsheet), but strategic organization and design makes all the difference.

The research on how smartphones have affected human attention spans is still unfolding, but scarily enough, a 2015 study found that it's decreased to eight seconds and it's debilitated reading comprehension.[1]

What is often labeled "multitasking" actually isn't quite the right word for what we do; what it means now, is switching rapidly between tasks — and ultimately getting less done[2]. Oh, and it's important to point out that people don't read— they skim, (according to a study cited in the *Guardian*.[3])

Don't get me wrong: I'm all on board with the current state of smartphones and in their future incarnations. They amplify our ability to perform certain tasks, to communicate with each other, and to access information. But as any entrepreneur (or, let's be honest, parent) knows, instant gratification isn't always the optimal solution.

We want viewers to readily check out the signage again, especially in environments with frequent repeated foot traffic. That's why it's important to not only get that message across in the instant, but also to build trust in the viewer so he or she intentionally chooses to look back to the signage in the future.

There's a really cool exception to this concept: Interactive kiosks. Users who approach these kiosks are already primed to discover and receive information, which means that there's more wiggle room to go denser or more data-heavy.

Another exception is sales or call centers, when employees are mostly stationary in a sales bullpen or call center cubicle; in this environment, we can display key performance indicators (KPI's) on the wall, as well as other relevant info, such as average call time or sales closed that day, in the main call or sales center.

VULNERABILITY IS A VALUABLE ASSET

We talked a bit about the inherent competition with personal devices. That brings us to our next big point: People should be in a *vulnerable* state when they're looking at our signs. That doesn't mean we're priming them to be pickpocketed; it means they're alert but not distracted by their phones or laptop. Their eye line is clear, and they're subconsciously ready to engage which the next piece of visual information that comes their way. They're almost looking for a distraction from their inner monologue.

Certain physical locations see more people in vulnerable states than others. We identify those locations to determine which ones are most ideal for a digital signage installation. We call these A+ locations **"transitional spaces."**

Hallways and certain areas of lobbies can be great picks. Spots near parking lot exits, elevator areas, conference rooms, bathrooms, and break rooms are also prime territory. These are spots where a person is less likely to be engaged with their phones or computers — they're en route somewhere, so they have less incentive to look down. They've got to be looking up and around, if not to complete their task, then to avoid crashing into other people.

Digital Books located in lobbies and waiting areas throughout the Ohio State University Medical Center improve patient experiences.

This general concept explains why magazine racks in grocery stores have remained in the same location for decades: Right next to the line. You're primed to complete a task — paying for your items — so you're probably not going to be looking at emails. Print magazines, for all of their shortcomings, have mastered the art of being mini-billboards.

The untrained eye might think a tabloid cover is a complete jumbled mess, but take a better look: Everything is carefully organized and consistent, usually with one large, attention-grabbing primary image dominating the page and three smaller, secondary headlines that keep the reader interested even after he or she's finished reading the main headline.

Break rooms where you're too busy making coffee to check your phone, conference rooms where you're slipping your phone into your pocket, blank walls just outside of the bathroom: These are all prime locations for digital signage.

It's all about finding your audience in that vulnerable state, where they're not already looking at a personal screen that's already completely customized to their own interests. It's difficult to compete with a phone already bursting with information that the user handpicked to consume. Digital signage can still win out, but it's a tougher battle.

Depending on the space, you may also have to compete with in-person interactions well as other digital media displays. And we know that those human-to-human conversations are important: Our goal has never been to replace verbal communication with digital. That's why we typically opt to place screens *outside* conference or meeting rooms, not within them, where people are gathering.

That said, in those transitional spaces we like, we see that digital screens fare well even when people are also engaging with each other. It's easy to glance at a large screen while remaining in conversation with another person, and doing so is markedly less rude than looking down at a cell phone. Digital signage becomes part of the environment, and if the messaging is done well, the person-to-screen interaction is no interruption at all.

Interactive Video Wall at the OSUMC Jameson Crane Sports Medical Institute. Visitors can individually engage with the content by using a tablet positioned in front of the wall.

Another key to audience retention and growth is to think out of the box with the entertainment value of the message you're delivering. Finding a novel way to deliver not-so-novel information can compensate for the lack of inherent excitement. This is something we at Industry Weapon think about constantly — how can we up the ante? How do we create a visual display that's genuinely fresh? — but you have a leg up on this challenge because you already know your own audience. You know their ages, their personalities and their interests, and you can leverage your understanding of your demographic.

With narrowcasting platforms, in contrast to smartphones or laptops, the viewer doesn't have a preexisting reason or intention to look at digital signage. Rather, the viewer happens upon the signage. Our job is to pique the interest in a meaningful way. Keep this in mind as we move into our next chapter, where we'll deep-dive even further into design, data, and communications.

A FEW THOUGHTS ON THE SUBCONSCIOUS MIND

Each second, the brains processes 11 million bits of sensory information, but only about a hundred of those bits manage to reach our conscious minds. So, where does the rest of that info go? The subconscious mind.

An incredible 95% of our thoughts and emotions occur in the subconscious long before we are ever aware of them, experts say. Digital signage allows brands to tap into the deeper levels of consciousness. By displaying attractive, repetitive, and dynamic content, messages are embedded into the viewer's subconscious mind.

There are three minds that work together every moment of your life: The conscious, the subconscious and the unconscious. And the differences between these three concepts are crucial. Right now, you're consciously reading this book. Take a second to look around. What items do you notice on your desk? Look at your shoe. Is it untied? By the way, are you hungry?

These are the mental functions of the conscious mind. Your conscious mind is that voice in your head that handles your present awareness — your real-time, in-the moment-thoughts. You're no stranger to this voice and its opinions. It has been interpreting the data given to you in real time for your entire life.

That means that the *subconscious mind* is what's responsible for almost everything we think and feel, including what we buy. In fact, 90% of purchasing decisions are made subconsciously. The subconscious mind is an infinitely vast storage space of everything we see, hear, and experience. When the conscious mind cannot process all of the information in a given situation, the subconscious takes over.

Now onto the unconscious mind, which is made up of your long-term memory storage and your instincts and drives. It contains all of the mental programs that you've had since birth. Your behaviors are based off of the patterns and beliefs stored in the unconscious mind. The unconscious mind is constantly communicating with the conscious mind through your subconscious mind. These communications come in the form of feelings, emotions, and dreams.

Got all that? It's a lot to comprehend, but it's nothing compared to what your brain is constantly processing, day in and day out. Let's consider what other people are thinking about right now. Inside an office, the typical employee is thinking about the email on his or her computer screen, the client sitting across from them in a meeting, the lunch that's long overdue. In retail, consumer thoughts can be more varied, but among their shopping-related thoughts, they're also paying attention to texts conversations, item prices and (again) food.

To break people's natural concentration on these other subjects, you first need to tap into their conscious minds. Colorful, bright, moving images are rudimentary ways of attracting attention. With digital signage, messages are delivered via moving images and visually appealing designs. Repetition takes messages and images that would tossed to the forgotten bin, and places them in the subconscious mind.

There, the messages can easily transfer to the conscious mind. It sounds like witchcraft, but it's simply exercising the effectiveness of repetitive content. Email communications and bulletin board posts are read once, then almost certainly disregarded in all three minds. Digital signage, on the other hand, is a constantly present medium that cycles communications to be played as often as needed until the message really resonates.

FUN + HABITS + IMPACT = TRUST

When schools, businesses, hospitals and other facilities start talking about installing a functional, effective security solution, the first thing they tend to do is test alerts on their digital signage screens. What they don't realize is that, no matter how seamlessly those tests appear to go, they skipped right over a crucial step: Establishing to the audience that these screens are a trusted source of information.

It's all about creating that perfect mix of "fun" and "habits" to deliver impact. Industry Weapon provides daily-curated programming that blends positive, useful daily information that trains viewers to take a look at the signage every so often during their regular routines. Think time, weather -- bite-sized chunks of information that people grow accustomed to seeing. When this is done correctly, the signage in turn becomes what we call a trusted screen. This way, in the unfortunate event that an emergency alert is, in fact, deployed, the audience isn't surprised or confused by the sudden relevance of the surrounding digital signage.

As soon as the signage becomes a trusted screen, that's when we can start to have a real impact. This programming starts the foundation of how we're going to boost engagement, and it's also how we're going to ensure that in unseen circumstances, people have the information they need as soon as they need it.

Here's an example of what that looks like in action: We work with several Goodwill locations that use a "color of the week" to signify to customers that certain products are new arrivals or just-discounted pieces. These product selections rotate on a 4-week sequence so the color of the week is certain to indicate a refreshed inventory. When frequent thrifters arrive at the store, they immediately know to check the color of the week, and they want to be able to see that information from anywhere in the entire location. By branding the color of the week on digital displays throughout the store (and maintaining that color on-screen at all times), we created a habit with Goodwill customers: They enter to shop and habitually check the screens. On top of that, because the color is only one asset of the two we require in our framework, there's other content on the screen providing other engaging information for the customer.

Even if this concept feels a bit foreign to you, I guarantee you already make use of it in your own life. Need proof? When you're headed to the airport to catch a flight, you have flight data available right on your phone. But even though those updates are right at your fingertips, you know to immediately check the constantly-refreshing digital screens in the terminal to confirm your flight status and gate. That's because you know those screens are managed up to the minute, and you (wisely) know that your phone could potentially be showing old data. You trust that the information onscreen is the most likely to be correct. You're also acting on a lifelong habit of checking those flight boards; you've been doing that your whole life, starting long before smartphones were in the picture. Your familiarity with the repeated process has built an important sentiment of trust toward these digital screens.

KEY POINTS:

- **Medium matters.** The large-scale video wall is not interchangeable with, nor an extension of, your company website, YouTube channel or email newsletter. It is its own unique platform, and it performs best when treated as such. This is even more important when you're working with interactive touchscreen kiosks, which have their own unique uses and capabilities.

- **Placement is prime.** In order to optimize engagement, place narrowcasting digital signage in transitional spaces where people are likely to be in a vulnerable state. That means they're not already looking at their smartphones or computer screens.

- **Keep it concise.** Brief, aesthetically-appealing bursts of visual information are far superior to intimidating walls of data or text. The exception is in call or sales centers, where Key Performance Indicators (KPI's) are appropriate for direct narrowcasting. But even in that environment, the data should be displayed in a visually attractive, digestible way.

KEY TERMS:

- **Transitional space,** an ideal place for digital signage. This is any location where people are moving from one static location to another, or are switching from one task to another, and are typically not looking at their mobile devices.

- **Vulnerable state,** the ideal state in which to find your potential viewer. This essentially means that they are not already engaged with another piece of digital media through their laptop or smartphone, and instead are primed to receive visual information.

* **Narrowcasting,** a targeted message to a limited audience, as opposed to a broadcast, which his sent out to all systems with certain specifications.

FURTHER READING:

The Medium is the Message: http://web.mit.edu/allanmc/www/mcluhan.mediummessage.pdf

Skim reading is the new normal: https://www.theguardian.com/commentisfree/2018/aug/25/skim-reading-new-normal-maryanne-wolf

Psychology of Good Signage: https://www.entrepreneur.com/article/295082

Myth of Multitasking: https://www.psychologyto-day.com/us/blog/creativity-without-borders/201405/the-myth-multitasking

Are Smartphones Shortening Our Attention Spans?: https://universityobserver.ie/are-smartphones-shortening-our-attention-spans/

Are Smartphones Making us Dumber?: https://www.forbes.com/sites/netapp/2012/09/12/is-an-digital-data-over-load-shortening-our-attentions-spans-and-making-us-dumb-er/#2c3ae00a1569

Microsoft Canada's Attention Spans Research Report: https://www.scribd.com/document/265348695/Microsoft-Attention-Spans-Research-Report

CHAPTER 2

MASTERING THE AUDIENCE ENGAGEMENT FRAMEWORK

It's a question that, too often, is literally life-or-death: How do we get people to look up from their cell phones?

I'm not being hyperbolic. From fatal car crashes linked to texting to the unimaginable number of people who've fallen off cliffs and waterfalls trying to snap the perfect selfie, the public has made it clear that they're resistant to ever putting their phones away. So, the question remains: How do we make our digital signage devices as attractive as the one in your pocket? And how do we defeat that incredibly tough competition?

To begin resolving this conundrum, we start by thinking about existing situations that force people to look up. One example: Ordering at a restaurant. Each and every person has to read the menu, and then — unless they really have no manners — they'll have to look at the waitress and speak. There are plenty of other daily instances like this that we don't tend to notice, since we're so used to them. From there, it's an advertiser's job to capture the audience's attention and deliver information.

THE AUDIENCE ENGAGEMENT FRAMEWORK™

A clearly defined structure which makes up today's most successful digital communications deployments

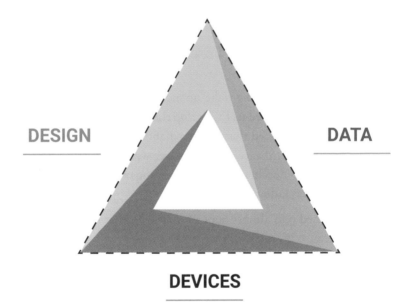

DESIGN

DATA

DEVICES

3 KEYS TO BATTLE DIGITAL IRRELEVANCE

In 2018 I gave a seminar titled *3 Easy Steps to Battle Digital Irrelevance*. It outlines the the three-part process of Industry Weapon's Audience Engagement Framework. This is our high-level, go-to battle plan when developing a strategy for a client, and these are the first steps we walk them through when developing a new client's strategy.

With these foundational points in mind, we've managed to flip failing digital signage strategies into ones that not only begin to tread water, but thrive. The three components to that strategy are **Design**, **Data**, and **Devices**. We're going to touch on each one briefly here, before deep-diving into each component in later chapters.

I still remember the big wake-up moment early on at Industry Weapon that, in time, led us to develop the Audience Engagement Framework. We realized that we were handing clients these powerful tools, both hardware and software, without ensuring that the client had a comprehensive understanding of how to effectively leverage them for audience engagement.

As it turned out, almost none of them had that innate knowledge — because it's not really an understanding that just occurs to people, even incredibly business- and advertising-savvy ones! Audience engagement encompasses a process of deliberate strategies that aren't too complicated, but they also aren't immediately obvious.

Of course, many clients figured they had it all under control. They already had a Content Management System (CMS) in place, and therefore were used to putting branded content through a system. The problem was, they were jumping straight to "How do I use this software?" rather than "How do I optimize content for this medium?" It's very similar to the novice mistake we talked about in Chapter 1, where people frequently think their digital signage should be used just like your everyday big-screen TV.

So, with these common mistakes and misunderstandings in mind, we developed the Audience Engagement Framework, which is an excellent starter guide to using digital signage to your advantage.

DESIGNING VISUALS FOR ENGAGEMENT

The design component of the Audience Engagement Framework can profoundly affect clients' design choices for the better. Design is one of the first topics we cover with new clients, and most people realize that design is best left to, well, designers! There's room for collaboration, and sometimes clients do want total control over their visuals, but few are totally unreceptive to our excellent in-house design team — especially once they see their work in action.

A remarkable 46.1% of people say a company's design is the number one criterion for discerning their credibility. If a company's content looks messy, consumers instinctively assume the same of their products and services. That's just not a risk that any business can afford to take. Think of it this way: When your kitchen countertop is a chaotic mess of loose papers, dirty dishes and stray bananas, it's impossible to find your keys; but when everything's nice and organized, you can grab them and get out the door. Graphic design works the same way: It helps viewers digest the information while putting in minimal effort.

There are four quadrants of visual engagement. We'll cover each of these components in detail in our next chapter; for now, a quick overview will suffice:

MOTION

The first component is motion. Clients frequently miss this one, as "signs" are generally thought of as a static medium. However, visual motion — done *appropriately*, not obnoxiously — is one of the surest ways to catch someone's eye. Rather than streaming a static slideshow, which tends to look dated in addition to boring, make use of video and animation. The motion doesn't necessarily have to come from the content itself; for example, an Instagram feed that's constantly refreshing might be complemented by a subtly spinning logo.

VISUALS

The second component is visuals. We want at least two separate visual assets on-screen at any time. This way, a viewer who's not interested in the first piece of content can make an immediate switch to the second. (This comes more naturally than ever these days, since everybody's brains are so used to quickly switching between website tabs and apps.) This is psychologically essential to successful digital content.

Non Compliant
At first glance, this slide appears to have two visuals but they are all aligned with the same topic.

Compliant
Something as simple as the current weather, date and time, when added to the slide adds a secondary visual to attract more eyes.

Not only is there a better chance that the viewer will find the content engaging, but the time it takes him or her to register the second piece of content will probably keep the eye locked long enough to see the next page. By that point, the person has become a fully-engaged viewer who's now seen at least four pieces of your content.

TIME

The third component is time. We've determined, after trying all sorts of variations, that the ideal time to have an asset onscreen is no less than four seconds. Any shorter than that is too brief for an audience member to register and care about; too much longer, and the content already starts to feel stale (wild, right? No wonder print publications are struggling). This means, if you have two assets on screen, eight seconds total is just about the perfect length of time.

The exception here is video clips, which we find should be played in their entirety — but long videos, like more than two full minutes, should almost always be avoided. Think about it: Who, really, is going to stand still and watch a video for two full minutes, especially when there's no audio? That's why sixty-second promotional spots are frequently edited into 30- and 15-second versions for different digital players. Recently, there's even been some experimentation with 6-second edits for social media (*"Creativity in Constraint"*), which likely stemmed from the success of the app Vine.

COLOR

The final component is color. While we try to stick to brand guidelines for color, we also know that certain colors can provoke strong emotional responses, which we reserve for specialized messaging. For example, an emergency message should flash on-screen in red or yellow, even (or especially) for a company whose colors are blue and white.

THE AUDIENCE ENGAGEMENT FRAMEWORK™

A clearly defined structure which makes up today's most successful digital communications deployments

DESIGNING VISUALS TO MAXIMIZE ENGAGEMENT

MOTION

There must be motion on the screen at all times

Why?
Critical to attract viewer's attention

VISUALS

At least two separate visual assets on the screen at once

Why?
A single message may not resonate with the viewer

TIME

4 seconds per asset

Why?
Long enough to engage, not too long to bore

COLOR

Choose colors that provoke strong emotional response

Why?
Specific colors inspire action

THE DATA CONTENT RATIO

Incorporating data into digital signage can be intimidating for new users — especially those who don't have much experience in using advanced data technologies. People often fall on one of two opposite ends of the spectrum in data strategy. Some people are completely resistant to using it all: *It's too much intricate information. I'd rather just deploy "relatable," generic content that anybody at all can understand.*

On the flip side, some users get a bit too excited about using data. Some like to use semi-hidden cameras that analyze people walking by the signage, and the messaging changes in real-time to something an algorithm deems relevant to that person. These are the Facebooks and Amazons of the world — parties that collect your search engine information and process it so that the next time you refresh the page, you're seeing advertisements for the vitamin supplement you just Googled. It feels invasive, like viewers are under surveillance, with messaging getting way too personal, too quickly.

At Industry Weapon, we find that there is a highly effective middle ground. We're using data to determine our messaging, but not in an invasive or troubling way. The user gets to see optimized results without compromising viewer privacy.

Your core message, whether that's brand messaging, sales, or productivity, should only be on-screen about 30% of the time. The other 70% should be what I call **Personally Relevant Content**, or Socially Relevant Content. Some clients are resistant to this idea, so let me explain what it looks like in action.

One of my favorite examples comes from a client we worked with awhile back — an aftermarket auto parts retailer. We integrated personally relevant content using data in two ways. First, we analyzed what people tend to come into the store looking for. After determining that about 80 to 90 percent of people who head into auto parts stores are in search of engine oil, it was easy to conclude that that specific product should be featured in the majority of the messaging. The digital content can, for example, direct customers to the right aisle, advertise the particular brands you have in stock, or promote a sale on the products.

Here's the second way we used data to craft personally relevant content. By equipping the signage with, essentially, an internal weather app, the display automatically modifies to advertise accordingly. If it's raining outside, the chances that someone's coming into buy wiper blades shoots up. The algorithm can determine, then, that it makes more sense to advertise wiper blades instead of wax. It seems simple, and that's because it is, but this small feature boosts sales and improves customer experience. It's all about integrating data in a way that makes sense for both you and your viewers.

A slightly higher-level example would be a call, sales, or manufacturing center. We work with these types of facilities often, and a common mistake we see is an illogical use of the data. There are too many metrics on the board — so many that no one would bother taking the time to read them — or the metrics are too high-level for the average line worker to really care about, like total gross or net profit. Those figures aren't meaningful to people on the production floor.

Instead, we use the data to deploy content relevant to the viewers, like units produced that day, or call time spent in queue. These are figures that an individual worker cares about. A progress bar might show whether or not he's likely to have to stay overtime, and who wouldn't want to know that info as far in advance as possible? In the case study at the end of this chapter, we'll look at how a medical technology manufacturer improved efficiency by taking these data strategy steps.

THE AUDIENCE ENGAGEMENT FRAMEWORK™

A clearly defined structure which makes up today's most successful digital communications deployments

THE DATA CONTENT RATIO

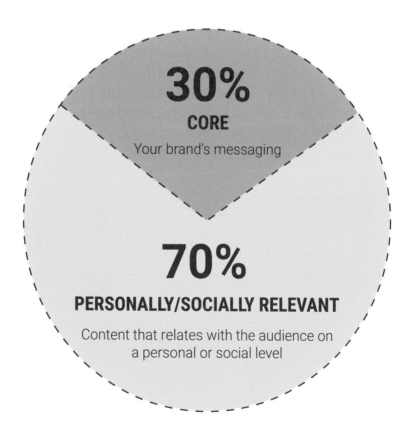

30%
CORE
Your brand's messaging

70%
PERSONALLY/SOCIALLY RELEVANT
Content that relates with the audience on a personal or social level

QUICK TIPS: EFFECTIVELY INCORPORATING INSTAGRAM INTO YOUR DESIGN

A few years back, the digital signage industry got a bit too excited about Instagram, Twitter and Facebook. Basic coding made it possible to easily program social media feeds onto screens, live-broadcasting pics and hashtags for all to see. The problem there is that social media is inherently designed for individual users. Instagram, for example, has a fresh, clean format — when you're looking at it by yourself on a phone. When you toss a bunch of Instagrams up on a much larger screen, things get muddy fast.

It's a lesson that's taken some time to learn in the digital space, but great design is non-negotiable. Think about your traditional clothing store. It's lined with carefully-chosen printed materials of models wearing the latest pieces. The storefront windows feature huge, static images in nicely-coordinated seasonal colors. It's an intentional strategic process that's been perfected over decades, so we shouldn't be surprised that digital signage needed some time to catch up.

Social media is sticking around, so you should absolutely integrate it into your digital signage solution. But strategy is everything. When it's overwhelming, it's a mess — but when you show off social media in a beautifully-designed way, your customers will enjoy the content as much as you do.

Do: Keep It Clean. "Quality, not quantity" gets overused, but it's a particularly important refrain when we're determining how to capitalize on social media content. There's just so much to choose from — tweets and photos and posts, oh my! — it's tempting to let 'em all scroll through in a jumbled collage and hope customers take the time to register it all.

Don't: Post Just Anything. All those huge printed materials we were just talking about? The models posed for hundreds, if not thousands, of photos during an hour-long shoot. Only the very best were chosen to be blown up for the storefront windows. Adopt that same process for your social media curation. There's no reason to show every last photo. Take the time to select the best content for your digital signage, just as you would for something you'd print.

Do: Think Outside the Box. It's also a great idea to think out-of-the-box. We've all seen tweets roll through in a line. Surely there's a better way to showcase particularly awesome quotes. Justin Garrity, a VP at our client Sprinklr, recalled layering tweets over a gorgeous professional food photography at a restaurant. Those images are much better than social media pics of a hamburger, but the tweets add a real-world personal touch.

THE PURPOSE OF DEVICES

When you combine data and design, you create a digital story. The data provides you with the information you want to share, and the design element encompasses how you actually share it. Once this digital story is prepared, it's time to determine the third part of the audience engagement framework: The device. The type of story you want to tell helps determine what set of devices will work best.

The digital device is the medium through which you're delivering your company's story. Your approach to devices should be holistic — bigger and more advanced are not always better, and not every type of business requires, for example, multiple highly-programmed interactive kiosks. A large, non-interactive video wall might actually be a better choice for telling your company's story. Other considerations, such as physical or technical limitations of the store itself, might come into play as well.

This is our number one criterion: The purpose of the device. The next criterion we look at is availability and redundancy. We don't want any piece of the strategy to be so specialty that it can't be replaced at the drop of a hat. Client needs can change very quickly, and so can device capabilities and technology. That's why it's ideal to have at least two options for each device, whether that's two different models from the same brand, or two equivalent models across brands. In the event that something malfunctions, or — more likely — just doesn't quite make sense for your re-imagined strategy, we can replace it with minimal headaches. More on device strategy is covered in Chapter 5.

Here's an example of why device purpose matters so much: We worked with the owner of a large restaurant who needed a model that could not only project menu items, but also transform to run a brand animation or other video content during off-hours or when customers were between orders. Here the redundancy was especially important, because there's no downtime in the food service industry.

If you lose the ability to project your menu items, you lose the sale. We needed something that was replaceable, but also versatile enough to run both those menu items and branded video content. As such, we implemented a particular type of advanced video screen with an embedded processor powerful enough to run the branded content on its own, but also capable of external streaming.

One of the coolest uses of devices we've seen came from athletic retail powerhouse Finish Line. Together we implemented interactive screens that reacted to the display shoes each consumer picked up while browsing. We set up an RFID reader in the display and a chip in each of the display shoes. When the particular shoe was placed on the console, relevant content, such as product information and video, as well as local social media mentions of the product, would instantly show up on the video wall.

It's a clever use of data and design, taking existing content and beaming it to the screen, but even better, it's insanely cool because it's personally relevant in a direct but non-invasive way. It's more advanced than the signage used in the auto parts retailer we talked about earlier. Instead of a read of the weather or general demographics, it's reacting in real time to the consumer's interest — but the consumer still, correctly, feels like he or she is in control of the situation. It's a reciprocal relationship: The customer picking up the physical shoe and the machine is showing the relevant content. It isn't some creepy digital box reading search history or analyzing buying patterns without customer consent.

I want to also touch on the social media component. Because the customer could see real-time mentions of the product, he or she is empowered to make an educated buying decision. Not only do shoppers see Finish Line's authorized branded content, but they also saw what real people in their community were saying about the shoe. This increases brand trust, which is crucial for customer retention. It plays into a strategy we'll discuss more in Chapter 6, called VOICE, or Verifiable Open Information for Consumer Enlightenment.

Of course, not everyone needs a custom RFID display for their store. Some (many!) just need, for example, a set of three displays with wireless capabilities or a video wall that can pivot quickly from menu items to brand content. The best part about the Audience Engagement Framework is that it's holistic and adaptive. Whatever the client's needs are, the Framework can adapt to meet them.

Finish Line Interactive shoe wall using RFID technology

BRINGING DIGITAL PURPOSE INTO HEALTHCARE

I really love working in the healthcare space. When we first got started in healthcare, the immediate digital signage need was obvious: Wayfinding. There are so many people coming through the facilities -- caregivers, other personnel, patients, visitors -- and successfully getting them to where they need to go is no insignificant challenge. But after getting wayfinding squared away, there's so much more to do, and it's been incredibly rewarding learning more about the remarkable people who work in our healthcare system and figuring out how digital signage can improve their work lives.

Getting to know the administrative personnel was a real wake-up call. These are individuals who work day in and day out in a tough environment and often go pretty under-appreciated. What's great about the technology is that we can give back to these caregivers, the people who have a huge impact on patients' well-beings, and give them the time, energy and focus that they've been lacking. There's a ton of extra work that gets piled onto these staffers, and many of those tasks can be alleviated with just a bit of digital signage assistance. We can utilize the technology to reduce that workload and give caregivers that much more ability to do the more impactful parts of their jobs.

We call them "caregiver boards," and they're used strategically, customized by purpose in order to deliver the most amount of value. For example, when a caregiver enters a room, he or she can take a look at a board to learn a patient's dietary restrictions, medication requirements, how many visitors have stopped by -- all information that typically requires tons of extraneous paperwork to sift through and decipher. Caregiver boards on the back of house and outside of rooms help caregivers know what the actual scheduled discharge date is so that nurses and doctors are aware of the actual discharge time. Hospitals lose millions each year when patients are discharged after the geometric mean length of stay (GMLOS) prescribed for a specific condition. More often than not, the length of stay gets extended due to miscommunication or lack of awareness of the actual discharge time. Using digital screens and color coded messaging helps keep doctors and nurses in the know and reduce lost revenues due to unnecessary extended hospital stays. By leveraging digital signage to serve this purpose, we save personnel time, help patients stay on track with their specific form of care, and reduce wasteful costs all-around.

To me, this is really powerful: Utilizing the environment in a way that benefits caregivers, patients and the healthcare facility as a whole.

We've also got other tools that we love to install in healthcare facilities, like donor walls. Donor walls are high-impact, large format interactive displays that showcase all the big donors who have made a major impact on the hospital or health system. These displays use video and imagery to give the recognition people deserve. I also love microdonor walls, which highlight real-time smaller contributions. Everyday people inside the facility are able to make donations and then see their name in lights as the video wall or display celebrates the contribution.

CASE STUDY: ANGIODYNAMICS

One of my favorite case studies for the integration of data into a digital signage strategy comes from our work with AngioDynamics. AngioDynamics, a manufacturer of medical, surgical and diagnostic devices, has grown exponentially since its founding in 1988. This steady growth has been fueled by a strong focus on innovation in product development and manufacturing operations. However, AngioDynamics struggled in the 2000's to keep that growth and development moving. Implementing digital signage marked an incredible turning point on the production room floor.

THE TRIAL AND ERROR OF MANUFACTURING PRODUCTIVITY TOOLS

Management relied primarily on verbal and paper communications, facilitated during Gemba walks at the start of each shift, to share metrics about line efficiency, utilization, and KPIs. The company's manufacturing manager realized that the years-long practice of sharing internal information via printed paper just wasn't working.

Staffers were glancing at the sheets and moving on with their day, never really retaining the information, never using it to modify their strategies or perfect their processes. The problem goes without being said: Those facts and figures are important! They're textual breakdowns of the entire business — what's working well, what's falling flat. It's just about impossible to make necessary adjustments without a comprehensive understanding of key metrics.

The production manager realized that digital displays would keep site information top of mind for line workers. His team's initial digital signage attempts leveraged a browser to stream information, but it was difficult and time-consuming refresh the content each day. He asked the IT department to find a solution that could easily deploy metrics to the displays. They reached out to our partner, who suggested Industry Weapon and our highly-regarded CommandCenterHD program. Free training and technical support are a given from us, so the AngioDynamics leadership was quickly on board.

Finding the perfect digital signage setup for AngioDynamics took some time. While employees may not have particularly enjoyed receiving information on paper, it's also what they were used to. So determining what types of content needed to be up onscreen was a collaborative process: The manufacturing and IT managers listened to employee feedback and tweaked accordingly. This type of employee-to-manager communication is a really important step in the transition to digital process. Employees can offer critical insights that you wouldn't necessarily notice on your own.

"Board members that have visited the site since installing the digital signage have given us excellent feedback. They are impressed that the company has intuitively improved day-to-day processes with visual communication."

- Lucas Sauer-Jones, Distribution Manager, AngioDynamics

REAL-TIME DATA VISUALS REVOLUTIONIZE THE PRODUCTION FLOOR

AngioDynamics' new digital signage strategy greatly improved communication between management and line workers. In fact, it enabled stronger understanding of key metrics by line workers, many of whom later admitted they'd previously felt too intimidated or uninformed to ask about unclear data points. For years, these line workers never mentioned to management that they didn't fully grasp important information about their day-to-day work.

The beauty of digital signage technology is its ability to integrate with databases that track each step of the manufacturing process. This information can be automated to the signs to keep everyone updated. In other words, it's the best way to communicate informational messaging to your audiences without email or paper. Production metrics, inventory management, statistics about product quality, worker-performance, machine performance, quota tracking, and business performance can be updated in real time and automated to the screens.

As they began seeing these numbers on the screens throughout the work day, employees began asking excellent questions about how to interpret the data and use it to improve both individual and team productivity. Real-time metrics are great motivators to get through the day: They always play it straight, telling staff exactly how much progress your team has made and what's left to go.

They're a really good friend to have in the office, and not just for supervisors. We'd go ahead and argue that they're a best friend for employees. Why? Well, because as AngioDynamics explained to us, real-time metrics are the golden ticket for employees who (understandably!) want to go home and enjoy their free time out of the office.

"The biggest question we get on the floor is, 'Why am I on overtime?'" AngioDynamics' marketing manager told us.

With the constantly-updating schedule metrics displayed via digital signage, "in real time, they start to see their schedule decrease, and once they get to zero they get to go home. It's all in their control. It's decreasing, and they get to go home earlier."

This method also allows for extra transparency: Employees who don't work the standard 9-to-5 become distrustful of their managers when they have no idea how long they'll have to stay at work each day. With real-time metrics, they can get that impartial information so they always know exactly how much more work is to be done before they can clock out.

Static reporting is getting left behind, and for good reason. It's not accurate, it's not motivating and it's just not the way of 2019. We have the technology to know exactly how much progress has been made, and if you're not already taking full advantage of that option, you're taking it for granted — at your own disadvantage.

BUILDING MORALE IN AN ORGANIC WAY

Not long after the real-time metrics were introduced on AngioDynamics' production floor, staff, of their own accord, turned their daily line statistics into an internal competition among the lines. Not only did this initiate conversations between staff and management about techniques to improve their numbers, but it fostered genuinely fun energy on the floor. It's not a condescending or gimmicky method of gamification — it's earnest competition.

Competitive energy can be a rush. Managers need to recognize that the drive to achieve goals should be motivating, not infuriating. The whole point of internal competition is to add some excitement to the day — not to make it miserable. It can be a tricky line to walk, especially when your teams are driven by numbers. Perhaps it goes without saying, but goals should always, in one way or another, be within reach. That might mean that goals are occasionally modified after bandwidth is fairly evaluated.

Competition, when it's functioning correctly, will boost morale and add a feeling of team spirit to the workday. Don't use it to create more work for your employees. Allow it to grow in a natural way, and then guide it with the right system of real, genuine rewards. Consistent number communication is sure-fire tactic to speeding up productivity. Representing statistical information visually, and sharing data-based information in an appealing way has never been easier. So there's no excuse to have bored, depressed employees. Up their game with a challenge, and keep them on their toes with numeric evidence that everyone can see.

The comprehensive metrics aren't the only reason why morale has improved on the production floor. Investing in digital signage can also foster a feeling of workplace community that paper just can't convey. AngioDynamics had the incredible idea to film video spotlights of employees whose personal lives have been impacted by the company's products.

That kind of humanizing content simply doesn't come through as vividly on paper, and it certainly isn't as easy to distribute. With digital signage, employees can watch compelling content about their own colleagues whenever it's convenient for them, and in doing so, they learn a little bit more about the people with whom they spend a whole lot of their lives.

Abandoning paper in favor of digital signage may sound like a major move, but truthfully, it's one of the few things in life that's much easier *done* than *said*. Once you effectively deploy digital signage, you'll see — as AngioDynamics did — that employees are suddenly eager to pay attention and actually retain the information they deserve to know.

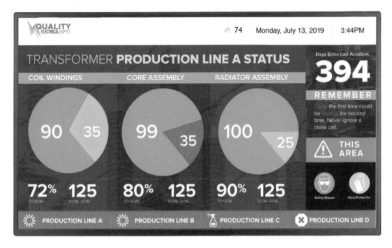

Typical Production Line KPI Board used within the manufacturing industry.

KEY TAKEAWAYS:

+ **The Audience Engagement Framework:** A digital signage strategy playbook developed by Industry Weapon. Its three parts are Design, Data, and Devices.

+ **Design:** IW's Design Strategy includes four parts: motion, visuals, time, and color. Static displays aren't eye-catching, but subtle motion corrects for that. The sweet spot is at least two visuals per slide and four seconds onscreen per asset. Keep brand guidelines for color in mind when developing your digital signage strategy.

+ **Data:** We find it's best to strike a healthy balance between zero data usage and "Big Brother"-level surveillance. A few key points of demographic information and optimization can really kick a digital strategy into high gear. Perhaps most importantly, messaging should be comprised of 30% core brand messaging and 70% socially relevant content.

+ **Devices:** Design and data determine the story you're going to tell, and devices are the tool you use to tell that story. Purpose, availability and limitations are our key parameters for determining which device is right for the job. For more on devices, see Chapter 5.

KEY TERMS:

+ **CMS (Content Management System):** The digital signage software platform inside of which content is created, managed, scheduled, and dispersed to the proper hardware.

+ **KPI (Key Performance Indicator):** These are defined data that are used to compare the success of an initiative, campaign, or program.

+ **RFID (Radio Frequency Identification):** A technology where digital data is read from electronic tags using radio waves.

+

FURTHER READING:

Google ad: https://www.thinkwithgoogle.com/marketing-resources/youtube-bumper-ads-six-second-storytelling/

AngioDynamics Business Impact Workshop: https://go.industryweapon.com/angiodynamics

Chapter 3

THE FOUR QUADRANTS OF VISUAL ENGAGEMENT

Ever experienced "death by PowerPoint?" This won't be too hard to imagine: You're in a meeting, and it's going on for too long. People are sneaking glances at their watches, their phones, belly button lint—whatever will offer a moment of reprieve. And *just* when it seems like it's about to end... the presenter fires up the projector and starts speaking over a PowerPoint. And not narrating in an engaging way, but reciting to you, bullet point-by-bullet point, each slide. And lest you think those slides are attractive, they're just on a bland stock template. There you have it: Death by PowerPoint. Unfortunately, many businesses that use digital signage suffer the same crushing effect. Here's how we resolve that.

In Chapter 2, I introduced the three parts of the Audience Engagement Framework: Design, Data, and Devices. Industry Weapon believes that with these three components working in tandem, we can get clients off to an amazing start in optimizing their business using digital signage. In this chapter, we'll cover specifically the design portion and its four quadrants of visual engagement.

▲	**THE AUDIENCE ENGAGEMENT FRAMEWORK**™
	A clearly defined structure which makes up today's most successful digital communications deployments

FOUR QUADRANTS OF VISUAL ENGAGEMENT

MOTION

There must be motion on the screen at all times

VISUALS

At least two separate visual assets on the screen at once

TIME

4 seconds per asset

COLOR

Choose colors that provoke strong emotional response

MOTION: THE MOVEMENT OF MEDIA

Arguably the most important element of digital signage design is motion. People traditionally associate the word "sign" with static entities, so motion often gets overlooked, even though it's actually one of the first boxes to check. Motion draws in the eye, as we're naturally geared to look at anything in our surrounding environment that's moving.

As corny as those sign spinners on the side of the road may look (and as overheated as they may be when they have to wear a giant animal costume), they're out there for a reason: They're more effective than a basic sign. It's simple evolutionary stuff, and it works. When you see something moving in your peripheral vision, you're going to notice it, even if it's on a subconscious level.

The general psychological principle we, and advertisers through most of the 20th century, are working on here is called "visual hierarchy," or the order in which you register objects in your environment. Color, shape, motion, and layout are all important here.

They determine both the order that you look at something within a piece of content, and whether you look at that content at all. Motion and color are paramount here for grabbing attention and distinguishing your signage from the rest of the visual landscape. Once your viewers are engaged, other components like visuals and time spent become more relevant factors.[4]

Many of our new clients who approach us with existing digital signage strategies are working with programming that's marginally better than a PowerPoint slideshow; sometimes, it is literally that. While PowerPoint (or Google Slides, or any comparable program) can be a useful tool to supplement a live presentation, it isn't sufficient on its own to deploy dynamic, engaging content. That's not what the software was designed to do, and even with integrations like video capabilities, it's not properly suited for these types of displays.

MOTION IN ACTION

Not long ago, we worked with a client whose team was initially a bit too jazzed about animation. After a bit of trial and error, they realized that while some subtle motion enhances the message, it's got to have purpose. Photos and text shouldn't bounce around for no reason. Everything that happens on screen should feel intentional and relevant.

The VP of User Research and Display at Sprinklr, an industry leader in data visualization, pointed out that when digital signage screens are constantly moving with animation, they become less pleasing to the eye — and the camera. People are constantly snapping photos, and a mid-animation shot of a display can totally hide the great marketing materials it's hosting.

"If you can take a photo with a screen in the background, and it makes a good photo, you know you have the screen right," he said. He added that no one should have to explain later on, "Oh, if you'd seen it, you'd know how it works." Digital signage should be understandable and attractive no matter what's currently on screen.

The idea of looking great in photos doesn't just apply to animation. It also means that no matter what's happening on the screen, it shouldn't be unclear what it's promoting. Maybe that means there's always a visible logo somewhere, or perhaps all the content adheres to a recognizable color scheme.

Digital signage is like a new piece of statement decor for your business. You wouldn't display a table that completely clashes with the whole room, and the same attitude should apply to your screens. Be sure to keep your animation subtle and your message clear.

VISUALS: SO VITAL, AND SO EASILY DONE WRONG

The second part of our design quadrant centers on the number of visuals. At least two visuals should be on the screen at all times. This calls back another very common early mistake: New clients often tell me they spend weeks slaving over a single visual, slide, or video clip. After all that work, when the content is finally displayed, engagement didn't move. That's frustrating!

The truth is, not every piece of content is going to be a hit. Even after careful research and revision, you're still going to have the occasional piece that doesn't quite resonate. (Although strategic data usage cuts down that chance by a whole lot.) That's why a second visual should always accompany the first. A viewer who isn't engaged with one piece of content will naturally switch to the second, often without even realizing it.

Visual thinking happens faster than text-based thinking. The message should already be narrowed down to the essentials: the who, what, where, when, or why. The visual elements, too, should be set up in a way that helps viewers easily understand the message. The design should not get in the way of the message, rather it should support the message in a visually appealing manner.

GRAPHIC DESIGN BASICS

You don't have to study advanced graphic design to grasp the core concepts of great visuals. One basic aspect to study is the layout. A simple rearrangement of the layout can make older content feel refreshed. This is useful when you have a standard message that you need to display for weeks, months or even permanently. Rearrange the visual elements of the campaign or choose new images and colors to complement the existing text.

Another quick lesson in graphic design? Be thoughtful about fonts. Text should stand out, not strain the eye of the viewer. Skilled graphic designers like Industry Weapon's in-house team have a more advanced understanding of fonts, but ultimately, there's one key rule that anyone and everyone can follow: The words must be easy to read. Sans-serif typefaces like Helvetica, Verdana and Futura are safe options that will be readable in any environment.

An easy to read sans-serif typeface like Helvetica, Arial, Verdana or Futura will translate well in any setting, and crisp, clean serif fonts like Georgia are also perfectly acceptable. Cursive-style fonts are much trickier to read and therefore tend to muddy a message.

Try to limit fonts to 2 or 3 different typefaces and styles per slide. This means that the body should all be one font and size, but the title can be something more experimental, so long as it's readable! Don't be afraid to choose fonts that are quite different from each other. Using two very-similar fonts can be distracting.

Spacing your visuals is perhaps the most important part of the process, and it doesn't come as naturally as you might think. Our clients rely on CommandCenterHD's built-in horizontal and vertical guides to keep everything aligned and sharp. Don't be afraid of white space! The eye needs to rest. Overstimulation won't elicit the desired results.

Tilly's combined multiple visuals, color and motion to show user generated content in its retail stores.

TIME: DISINTEREST IS NOTHING TO BE APATHETIC ABOUT

How much time should an asset remain on screen? We've had clients whose existing strategies sent images whizzing past with no time to register, and others who showcased sleepy slideshows of office photos and memos. We'll give a hard pass to both.

This is an easy one that doesn't require much further explanation: Four seconds per visual allows the viewer enough time to register what it is and process the information. If the display is effective, it'll hold on to the eye long enough to keep it watching through the next slide.

COLOR: CASTING THE EMOTIONAL TONE

Finally, we get to the most commonly-debated design element: Color. This is sometimes a sticking point for clients, as brands typically have a color scheme already in place. We like to stick to this color scheme as often as possible for visuals. After all, reinforcing brand standards is a good thing. However, we also know that certain colors can provoke emotional responses.

Ahead you'll find a graphic that outlines the emotions different colors provoke. You might not personally find them all to be true — and that's totally fine! Maybe the color orange doesn't quite say "creativity" to you, but I'd be willing to bet that the right shade of green, when folded into a campaign about company growth, gets the point across. Most of the color associations are pretty universal.

Like they always say, variety is the spice of life. Staying within the same palette category is fine, but don't use the same colors for all 17 of the slides in your campaign. The same colors time and time again might even look like one long slide to less-observant audience members. You might even want to jump from a slide with a blue background to a contrasting orange. The unexpected change catches the eye much like motion graphics do.

Sometimes it's wise to change up the color scheme to emphasize a real-time message that employees need to know right away. This is especially useful for our clients who have call or sales centers. We generally like to broadcast live KPI's here; however, if there's a work-related emergency, like our calls are falling below the SLA (Service Level Agreement) or there's something holding up the production line, we switch to a bright, eye-catching color for an attention-grabbing message.

More important, of course, than production issues are actual emergency situations. Red is typically the go-to color, and bold fonts accompanied by even bolder motion graphics are a necessity. It's also worth noting that we've worked with some clients to link their digital signage to alarms so both systems are working together when it matters most.

CASTING THE EMOTIONAL TONE

We've found that with an understanding of these four quadrants under their belts, clients are well-equipped to use digital signage to their advantage. Before we started training new clients with these guidelines, their content mirrored PowerPoint presentations and Excel spreadsheets. We quickly realized we needed to arm our clients with core design skills.

There's a fifth element to the four design quadrants that we like to throw in as a bonus: Entertainment. Some might consider it a "cheat" or a "hack" compared to straightforward brand messaging, but "infotainment" has become a proven genre of media, and the occasional usage of jokes, entertaining visual media, or other pure entertainment elements can prove to be great supplements to an already well-designed digital signage strategy.

THE EMOTIONS COLOR PROVOKES

Color	Emotion	Industry	Used To
RED	Excitement Energy Passion Courage Attention	Entertainment Food Sport Fire Protection Children's Products	Stimulate Create Urgency Draw Attention Caution Encourage
ORANGE	Optimistic Independent Adventurous Creativity Fun	Art Entertainment Food Sports Transportation	Stimulate Communicate Fun Draw Attention Express Freedom Fascinate
YELLOW	Enthusiasm Opportunity Spontanity Happiness Positivity	Food Sports Transportation Travel Leisure	Stimulate Encourage Relaxation Awake Awareness Energize Affect Mood
LIME GREEN	Growth Harmony Fertility Kindness Dependability	Environment Leisure Alternative Energy Entertainment Education	Restore Energy Promote Growth Nurture Rejuvenate
KELLY GREEN	Safety Harmony Stability Reliability Balance	Environment Banking Real Estate Farming Non-Profit	Relax Balance Revitalize Encourage Possess
SKY BLUE	Freedom Self Expression Trustworthy Wisdom Joy	Entertainment Communication Children's Products Technology Aerospace	Draw Attention Inspire Trust Suggest Precision Communicate Consciousness Stimulate Productivity

	Emotion	Industry	Used To
ROYAL BLUE	Trust Responsibility Honesty Loyalty Inner Security	Security Finance Technology Health Care Accounting	Reduce Stress Create Calmness Relax Secure Create Order
VIOLET	Imagination Spirituality Compassion Sensitivity Mystery	Humanitarian Psychic Religion	Encourage Creativity Inspire Combine Wisdom & Power Create Impression of Luxury Intuition
PINK	Compassion Love Immature Playful Admiration	Children's Products Woman's Products Beauty Fashion	Communicate Energy Increase Pulse Motivate Action Fascinate Encourage Creativity
BROWN	Reliability Stability Honesty Comfort Natural	Agriculture Construction Transportation Legal Food	Stabilize Imply Common Sense Suppress Emotions Create Warmth
GRAY	Neutral Practical Conservative Formal Quiet	All Industries Typically combined with other colors	Create Sense of Composure Depress Energy Communicate Maturation
BLACK	Power Control Authority Discipline Elegance	All Industries Typically combined with other colors	Hide Feelings Intimidate Radiate Authority Create Fear Associate with Mystery

CASE STUDY: COLLEGE OF THE CANYONS

College of the Canyons is a public community college in Santa Clarita that's rapidly grown from teaching several hundred students to more than 20,000 students each semester.

With such a large, constantly-expanding student population, using traditional communication methods proved fruitless as the school attempted to deliver important messages like campus announcements, scholarship updates and breaking alerts. Industry Weapon helped the college revamp its strategy using impactful design.

Upon first teaming up, we took inventory of what communications efforts were already in place. Emails went out frequently, but engagement was near-zero. Fliers and posters were fully ignored. Most interesting to us? Some form of digital signage had been functioning on campus for more than a decade, which is great — but the campaigns were produced in PowerPoint, and as we've already talked about, that system just isn't built for compelling design. The content that was static and bland. And on top of that, the administration had struggled to centralize the software, so creating the messaging was time-intensive and confusing to upload.

There was no clear ownership of the signage strategy, in part due to the counterintuitive and clunky software the administration was using. Because it was so difficult to use, messaging was, more often than not, noticeably outdated by the time it was published on-screen. The signage strategy was so lackluster that faculty almost always opted to use emails or papers taped to walls instead.

Without a gatekeeper for standards, communications felt disjointed and resulted in outdated content and disengaged viewers. The school's existing digital signage solution did not house a centralized operational structure. That didn't come as a major surprise to us because faculty members and administration already have demanding jobs. They don't have the time or energy to labor over content creation for digital displays that no one bothered to look at anyway.

> "We recognized early on that digital signage was a necessary communications tool. Very quickly it became apparent that centralized ownership was essential to ensure long term success."
>
> -Hsiawen Hull, College of the Canyons

College of the Canyons could see that their methods weren't working, so they attempted to utilize some free digital signage software available online. But the options required a lot of end-user labor, defeating the purpose of scaling the medium across campus to all departments. At one point, they invested in an expensive solution from an Industry Weapon competitor and were stunned to find that their software was even more confusing than the free online versions.

Somewhere along the line, we were called in, and our initial assessment didn't take long to compile as we took a look at their campaigns. It was a clear case of violating multiple quadrant "rules," misusing motion, visuals, and time. The good news is, the colors were kind of on brand — but that's a moot point since the programming was so unengaging that no one would ever notice them. Because of the convoluted software systems and lack of expertise among college staff, the information was never socially relevant, an issue easily resolvable by leveraging data systems.

Industry Weapon provided guidance on both design and software and eagerly replaced College of the Canyon's outdated signage and software. Now College of the Canyons broadcasts well-designed and engaging material based on Industry Weapon's Design Quadrant, and because of our free training and technical support, administration members responsible for communications are experts at using their digital signage software.

ANALYSIS:

College of the Canyons is an example I like to talk about because they already had some digital signage in place — for over a decade! — before we entered the picture. They were on the right track but had gotten a bit lost along the way. Even with those screens up and running, engagement was super low, with most students ultimately finding more value in print materials and emails.

This failing strategy was primarily rooted in two issues. First, design. CoC's strategy was initially based around PowerPoint, which produced visually unappealing campaigns that students and faculty readily ignored. The second problem is that even when viewers did notice the content, it was frequently outdated due to the use of archaic, convoluted software systems and lack of user expertise. Faculty members and administrators weren't able to update the signage programming because the software was too difficult to use.

Industry Weapon resolved the situation by providing guidance on both design and software as well as replacing the outdated software and systems with our own. Today, if you ever find yourself in Santa Clarita, take a look at the College of the Canyons campus. The lovely campus is accented by awesome digital signage that keeps students and staff in the know

KEY TAKEAWAYS:

- The Four Quadrants of Visual Engagement — Motion, Visuals, Time, and Color — make all the difference in the success of a visual campaign.
- Displaying multiple but complementary visuals keep the audience engaged, and cast a wider net for engagement.
- Four seconds is the ideal time per asset onscreen.

- Color should generally follow brand guidelines, but don't be afraid to deviate, especially for breaking alerts or particularly time-sensitive content.

- Entertainment is the "secret weapon" and the fifth quadrant for visual engagement. If you can engage your audience by genuinely entertaining them, the message is more likely to stick.

- Visual Hierarchy is a key principle in advertising. It describes the order in which the eye is drawn through images or features in an environment.

FURTHER READING:

Visual Hierarchy: https://www.theartsjournal.org/index.php/site/article/view/78/77

https://go.industryweapon.com/sprinklr

CHAPTER 4

VISUAL STORYTELLING

Earlier, we talked about how design and data come together to produce a brand story. In this chapter, I'm going to dive a little deeper into the *kinds* of imaginative, innovative stories you can tell with your digital signage strategies, and the change you can inspire inside your firm or company by doing so.

THE THREE TICKETS TO EMPLOYEE RETENTION

One of the most popular programs Industry Weapon has developed is our Three Steps to Employee Retention, which we've presented in seminars to pretty great responses. The "war on talent." a phrase coined by McKinsey in 1997, is relevant as ever today (*"The War on Talent is Real"*), and it's a tricky battle to approach.

Millennials are far more likely to switch jobs (or entire career paths) than their parents ever were. In fact, more than 70% are either not engaged or actively disengaged from their workplace, a recent Gallup poll showed. Digital signage is a cost-effective and intelligent solution for improving employee retention rates, facilitating a spirit of team-building, and cutting down on company hiring costs. (*"Millennials: The Job Hopping Generation"*).

For corporate communications, the three pillars of employee retention are **Publicize, Promote**, and **Project Vision.**

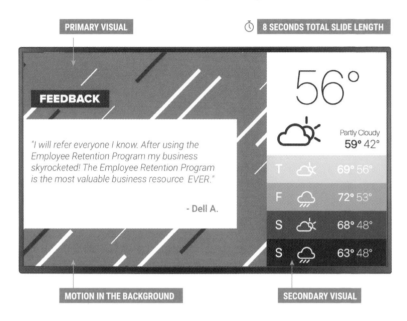

PUBLICIZE

Let's start here by clearing up a common misconception. Companies, especially those which frequently deal with sensitive documents and guarded information, tend to mistakenly think that "publicize" means broadcasting confidential information on screens throughout the workplace. That's certainly not advisable! "Publicize" means promoting exciting, publicly-available company accomplishments and developments. Throughout your organization, individual employees are working on their own cases, clients, initiatives and projects. And while those at the executive level are likely kept in the loop on big wins, often partners' everyday colleagues have no idea what's going on in the office next door.

Digital signage bridges that gap. By publicizing those great wins throughout the office, staff will not only feel more adequately acknowledged for their own hard work, but they'll also be able to see that the company is thriving on a larger scale. It fosters a sense of community and joint purpose in an often isolating environment.

PROMOTE

Just barely under pay and vacation time, a legitimate thank-you message is the third most valued sign of workplace appreciation, according to a 2017 OfficeTeam survey. In fact, two-thirds said they'd leave their jobs if they didn't feel adequately acknowledged in the office. Digital signage is a hassle-free but incredibly effective medium for proving to your employees that you recognize and care about them as human beings.

In all types of industries, there's a prevalent common negative sentiment of "To them, I'm just a number" — the idea that their worth is solely measured in black-and-white figures. Celebrate your people because they deserve it, and because their value to the company goes beyond their quarterly earnings or goal progress.

Showcase birthdays, employment anniversaries, or even personal milestones like welcoming a new baby or running a marathon. These digital announcements can be presented in non-intrusive and professional ways that enhance the workplace environment.

There's so much room for creativity here. Some of my favorite ideas require a bit of crowdsourcing, and you might be surprised by how eager employees are to contribute. I love seeing concepts like "20 Years Ago..." where the signage showcases throwback photos of employees from decades back. Your office may already have simple long-standing features, like a bulletin board featuring photos of employees' new babies. Why not show more recent family photos, like summer vacation snaps from across the company? You can also highlight specific employees with cool or unexpected hobbies, like that HR manager who also performs each Thursday in a punk band. Meaningful communities require deeper interpersonal knowledge than what clients you're all working on.

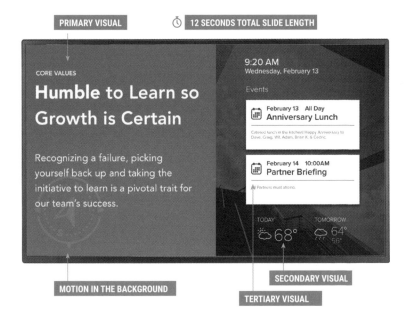

PROJECT VISION

Where are we headed? Certainly, information about overarching business goals and blueprints must be handled carefully, but your team should be in the know about initiatives that are safe for wider consumption. You likely have impressive plans in place that are no secret at all, but after that monthly all-hands meeting comes to a close, they're basically never mentioned again. This is especially true in larger enterprise organizations, where the leadership is typically far removed from day-to-day happenings.

Allow your digital signage displays to promote your company's vision for the future. This could mean, for example, showcasing a newly-revised mission statement. Do your employees really know what it means? Do they know why you chose it, and what it means for the months and years to come? Your team has a clear path forward, so it's crucial to ensure that your employees know where it's going.

We fold Publicize, Promote and Project Vision-based content into campaigns along with core messaging and socially relevant information. In turn, viewers come to see digital signs as genuinely useful, purpose-based devices from which they can glean important information.

GETTING A GRASP ON COMPANY CULTURE

I love the strategy developed by nonprofit Every Monday Matters, one of our partners, a company that delivers concise, impactful messaging that, through various means, empowers people to find value in their lives and in their work. Incorporating EMM into company programming and internal communications has proven groundbreaking for other brands from top to bottom, encouraging genuine personal empowerment on an individual level.

Different businesses have different vibes. A laid-back company culture isn't necessarily more enjoyable than a more buttoned-up one! If you don't already have a feel for your employees' personalities, and what drives them to work with you, it's most certainly time to figure that out.

What about your company attracts applicants in the first place? Why do hires stick around? What pleasure do they derive from their careers? Understanding what makes your employees tick will help you to develop engaging, meaningful communications that speak to them on a personal level.

While some of your messaging will be more corporate, programming like EMM's helps people reflect on and improve their own lives. Personal satisfaction is powerful. When people feel good about themselves, that translates into their work.

"If you can get someone to look at the challenges in their own life and see that they're temporary, they're not these things that are going to cripple them," explained David & Goliath CEO David Angelo, who helped integrate Every Monday Matters into his company's internal messaging. "You can instill values that give them permission to believe they're bigger than the challenge.

They're going to look at their clients the same way. So [business success] is a byproduct of what you're doing on the inside."

In addition to being aesthetically attractive, a great feature of digital signage is that it's so customizable and adaptable. You can tweak accordingly, redesigning as necessary until you feel like you're striking the tone that really encompasses and improves your company culture.

Authenticity can't be faked; it has to start from within. Employees who feel valued and inspired put that positive energy into creating a business that others find valuable and inspiring. Clients and customers are intuitive — they can sense when a company believes in its vision. When you make real internal changes to promote that vision, you'll start to truly see those results unfold.

HOW COMPANY CULTURE IMPACTS THE BOTTOM LINE

I want to take a minute to pause here and think about how digital signage can emphasize a healthy company culture. If you know your workplace has fostered an awesome sense of purpose and community, you should be really proud of that. I urge you to showcase it because it's a real accomplishment.

Great company culture and business growth go hand-in-hand. Happy people, better profits. Sounds pretty good, right? Many executives have been slow to recognize that a positive company culture doesn't just benefit employees: It contributes to healthier, more sustainable earnings.

Businesses across all industries have long struggled to figure out what, exactly, is the perfect recipe for a great workplace environment. Physical changes can go a long way; comfortable office chairs, inspired decor, perks like coffee bars and massage chairs, etc. But true culture is born from people themselves. No fancy products or cool perks can create the same genuine impact as real internal change.

As David Angelo put it during our conversation about his company's programming: "If we can make a difference in corporate culture and inspire people inside that culture to give their heart and soul toward everything they do there, the byproduct is going to be better products, better services, better relationships and a stronger bottom line."

An awesome concept — but how does it get put into action? It's not easy to bridge brand-new connections, effectively bettering the relationships employees have with each other, with the company, and with themselves.

A CLOSER LOOK: RETENTION IN LAW FIRMS

Digital Signage in Action in Paul Hastings' NY Offices

We've installed digital signage inside all types of organizations — retailers, college campuses, government organizations — but it's perhaps shown its greatest power in the battle against law firm turnover. Powering every great law firm is its people, and successful firms understand that top-tier talent is a valuable commodity. There's no real substitute for a partner with years of niche, fine-tuned expertise. That's why the rapid rate of turnover plaguing the legal field is so alarming: Day after day, remarkably skilled lawyers are walking away from their jobs — and sometimes their whole careers. It's a complicated issue, but our "Publicize, Promote and Project" strategy can alleviate and resolve major elements of the retention battle.

Industry Weapon has worked closely with firms ranging in size from small boutiques to massive global teams. The response has been overwhelmingly positive. Among the firms we've worked with is Paul Hastings, a leading international firm that works with top financial institutions and Fortune 500 companies. Steve Austin, an IT manager at Paul Hastings, told us that Industry Weapon's signage managed to "strengthen employee retention and dramatically cut down turnover costs."

Within the legal field, in particular, there's a common negative sentiment of "To them, I'm just a number" — the idea that their worth is solely measured in black-and-white figures. When we employ "Publicize, Promote and Project," partners and associates are constantly reminded of why they're there and how much they're valued. A former Paul Hastings exec lauded the Industry Weapon strategy here, telling us, "Most firms focus on the traditional approach to build loyalty, especially for the lateral partners. That's including financial incentives and other perks. A sense of partnership is somewhat lacking."

He added that by using our approach to digital signage, firms "have a chance to elevate internal recognition and strengthen a sense of belonging with more meaningful content delivered via messaging tools like [yours]."

In addition to broadcasting team goals and wins, it's important to emphasize human moments. Showcase birthdays, employment anniversaries, or even personal milestones like welcoming a new baby or running a marathon. These digital announcements can be presented in non-intrusive and professional ways that warm up the historically chilly law firm workplace environment.

CASE STUDY: HIGHWOODS PROPERTIES AND ORVIS

Working with real estate leader Highwoods Properties was an awesome lesson in figuring out what works and turning those elements up a notch. When we first met the Highwoods team, they revealed they'd tried out a number of different internal comms solutions. So we asked point-blank what works the best. The answer was immediate: "The Link," Highwoods' electronic newsletter that's deployed on digital signage in communal areas throughout its offices.

And while we'd love to take all the credit, the Link is just as much a vision of Highwoods' CEO, Edward Frisch. With nine divisions and 450 employees, Ed loved the idea of hosting an all-hands meeting with staff. But it just wasn't feasible to coordinate a time that worked for everyone.

So Ed focused on strategizing a way to equally communicate with everyone to really encourage that sense of community within the Highwoods walls. Even though Industry Weapon isn't as large as Highwoods, we instantly identified with this issue. It can be near-impossible to get everyone in one room — even for the yearly office holiday party. (Which always rocks.)

Sure, digital signage is useful for broadcasting company updates. But what really makes all the difference is the personal touches. That's crucial, and it's what business impact is all about. It's fun, it's creative, it allows the culture to actually surface from the employees and the celebrating that. You shouldn't have to *create* company culture. It's already there, so show it off. That's really cool when you're deploying your internal comms through multiple facilities, but it's also great even inside just one office.

"We found that people wanted to know more about what the divisions were doing, more of what the everyday man is doing. People like them," revealed Jenny Lavery, Highwoods' Marketing Coordinator. "They understand buildings — it's what they do every day. What else are they doing? What's our culture like?"

To that end, the team started brainstorming fun, lighthearted ideas inspired by their own existing company culture. Each employee was given their own Highwoods-branded "little blue man," a small figurine they could keep on their desks. The marketing team launched an idea: What if employees were encouraged to photograph their little guy as they traveled throughout the year?

Staffers loved the concept and were eager to submit their snapshots from vacations and events across the globe. The photos were then broadcast on the digital signage screens throughout each facility. What's the takeaway here? Once you find something that works, run with it! Push the envelope.

Also, while you should take internal comms seriously, if you're having fun, the rest of the company will too. Don't get too pushy on deadlines. Let the employee engagement come on its own time, and be flexible. There's a temptation to pull the cord quickly on ideas that don't immediately take off. But when you have a large audience, it really can take some time for messaging to blossom.

IT WORKED? TIME TO UP THE ANTE

The Highwoods team knew from their little blue man project that employees were eager to participate and genuinely engage. So the marketing team decided to unroll a major initiative. This thing took a whole lot of brainstorming, planning, and executing — but man, did it resonate.

"We asked every division to create a video pretending you're pitching *Jeff Bezos from Amazon* — what would you say about your division," Vicki explained. "We sent them a box: Here are some instructions, here are some tools to help you, like a clapboard, a microphone. And then we also said, here's another box of things you must include in the videos."

Inside that box? All sorts of goofy items, from Highwood-branded to totally random. And… an adult-sized dinosaur costume. It was a hit. Wait, that's an understatement…. It was a giganotosaurus hit. Each video incorporated the dinosaur costume in hilarious, bizarre ways. Employees had a total blast: "It just gave them a platform to use their creativity in a different way," Jenny said.

Across all types of industries, we've all, at times, needed to limit the amount of personality we show in a corporate environment. Light-hearted "missions" like Highwoods' bring some fun to the job. Projects like Highwoods' also show employees that you know they've got a tone of creativity, and you trust — and encourage! — them to use it.

SOCIALLY RELEVANT STORIES

Social media is everywhere, but as simple as our timelines may seem, it's a complicated landscape that can easily be misused in marketing. When utilized properly, one of the most exciting places to showcase social media is in the retail space. Several of our clients have requested integration of social media into their store digital signage, and the results have been fantastic.

Product reviews can make a splash, as can general Twitter or Instagram buzz around your product. See for yourself: Just search whatever posts are hashtagged or geotagged your brand, and you'll see how much opportunity is there. It's a very authentic and organic-feeling way to engage consumers with your brand both in and out of their shopping experience.

Don't make the mistake of whitewashing the content: In order to build trust, you should showcase all types of feedback (within reason). Consumers appreciate and respond to that type of transparency. Different brands are comfortable with different levels of "honesty" here; that is, you may want to employ some degree of content moderation. But we generally find that the brands that are less sanitized tend to see better engagement.

AUTHENTICITY IS EVERYTHING

Authenticity is an issue that so many businesses battle — and nearly as many are reluctant to admit it. Wouldn't it be simpler if we were all just building products and services for ourselves? Our own families in our own neighborhoods? The truth is, working to understand the customer is a complicated and constant task. That's especially true when your consumer base is wide-ranging

— you're attempting to cohesively market toward a huge swath of all different types of people.

Branding and authenticity go hand-in-hand. That's all we could think about as we arrived at the headquarters of one of our clients, sporting goods retailer Orvis, in Vermont. For decades upon decades, Orvis has polished its reputation as a premier high-end sporting goods company. And as soon as you enter the Orvis campus, you feel that. The entire beautiful green campus, despite being a place of business, is designed to promote its core mission: Get outdoors and enjoy life. We even did our Business Impact interview with CXO Dave Finnegan outside in the crisp fall air.

Think of the brands you appreciate the most, especially the ones you've loved since childhood. The Walt Disney Company is a classic example. Yes — no doubt about it — it's a profit-driven corporation. And it's run by adults, not children. But the brand has done a masterful job staying true to its image and showcasing leaders who embody its spirit. While nobody can quite capture the magic of Walt Disney himself, there's a clear pattern of highlighting execs who have a certain sparkle.

Demonstrating authenticity is trickier than it sounds. It can easily come off as corny and over-the-top, completely undermining the entire goal. That's one example of a discussion that unfolds at trade shows, where customer experience experts like Dave gather to share ideas and talk about what works — and what really, really doesn't.

A concept I like is "purity of motive equals purity of brand." At trade shows, people are usually eager to share their own learnings. And really, that's just another element of authenticity: Human-to-human discussions about the business, about branding, about customers. When people are working together in a genuine way, that absolutely bleeds into the brand. Customers can sense it.

The cross-channel customer experience excellence we've seen from Orvis is a product of the innovation, collaboration, and genuine love people have for this brand. The innovation comes from stellar employees. The collaboration comes from within and outside the company — insights from other industry leaders at trade shows have certainly helped the team fine-tune their concepts and designs — and the genuine love is a variable that can't be overlooked. It ties everything together with that critical sense of authenticity.

If you haven't yet made it out to a trade show for your industry, that's step one. Start meeting people who truly live the products they sell. They'll help you better understand your own business, and their passion will reinforce the love you feel for your own work.

CREATING PERSONALIZED EXPERIENCES

We'll talk more about leveraging social media in retail spaces in Chapter 6. For now, let's turn to another story of a signage strategy that was improved by focusing on a story that was socially relevant to the target audience.

Not long ago, we worked with a major casino brand to implement an interactive displays targeting high rollers. Those visitors are frequent guests who make repeat visits to the property, spending a lot of money at the attached restaurants and shops while playing their favorite games. This was a great lesson in trial-and-error. Initially, we missed the mark with our kiosk implementation. We programmed the screens to provide basic information, like where the different tables were located. The issue? The high rollers already knew this information because they visited so often. An interactive map of the casino didn't mean much to them.

It was a case of not quite understanding the audience, and even just a slight disconnect there can make all the difference. So we went back to the drawing board.

By compiling some basic background information, we allowed each guest to build an individual profile. Each one displays the visitor's first name, player level (i.e. silver, gold, platinum), their preferred games, and other customizable information. When the guest logs in, he or she is welcomed with a personalized screen: *Here are the tables available for your favorite game, here are the wait times at your favorite restaurants*, etc. Every once in a while we'll throw in a special deal on a restaurant or shop, like a simple exclusive limited time offer on drinks or food at the casino. (See Chapter 6 for more information about SEL as a sales and consumer engagement tool.)

While the core objective is to keep high-value players in the casino longer, enabling them to spend more money across the property, the kiosks don't only serve that agenda: They provide a genuine service to the user. It doesn't feel like a sale, and it doesn't feel intrusive. It's an opt-in system that's providing personally relevant information about a place the user already enjoys and frequents. As a visitor, you feel like this place, and the people behind it, understand and care about you.

Sometimes the best thing that can happen is to miss the mark. In this situation, we learned a whole lot from our misstep, and navigating to a solution helped us improve our subsequent programming in remarkable ways.

KEY TAKEAWAYS

+ Data and design are the keys to creating a visual story.
+ The best digital signage strategies work in tandem with their target audience. At Highwoods Properties, a highly interactive video strategy with employee participation proved to be wildly successful at boosting engagement. For our casino client, respecting and genuinely understanding audience needs was key to developing a winning strategy.

- The Three Pillars of Talent Retention are Publicize, Promote, and Project Vision. This three-step process helps employees realize that they are a part of a winning team, and they have a bright future within the organization. This plan has worked well across various disciplines and industries, and it's been especially successful inside law firms.

FURTHER READING:

https://www.inc.com/jacob-morgan/the-war-for-talent-its-real-heres-why-its-happening.html

https://www.gallup.com/workplace/231587/millennals-job-hopping-generation.aspx

https://go.industryweapon.com/highwoods

https://go.industryweapon.com/orvis

CHAPTER 5

TALKING TECH: UNDERSTANDING PURPOSE, LIMITATIONS, AND AVAILABILITY

Can the integration of technology inadvertently damage a brand? For those who are always a bit wary of advanced tech, the answer will come as no surprise: When implemented without strategy or thoughtful intention, technology can absolutely hinder business. But before we look at a compelling example of such a flounder, let's cover some overarching basics on devices.

Devices are the third component of our Audience Engagement Framework. Some prospective clients mistakenly think that because Industry Weapon is a software and technology company, we push tech above all else, with less regard for story or messaging. Of course, in reality, we know that type of approach leads to lackluster results, and that rolling out digital signage without a real plan can actually decrease sales and productivity. That's never what we want to see. The truth is, devices should serve as a medium for the story you're trying to tell — the story shouldn't be secondary to the screen. That's why our very first principle of device implementation is Purpose.

WHAT IS A PURPOSE-BASED DEVICE?

Devices are not one-size-fits-all — and that's why they're so fun. There are so many factors to consider, some of which can pose wild challenges for the Industry Weapon team. For example, we had one client who wanted to showcase a large video wall, comprised of five 65" screens. He envisioned a truly massive display that would to tell the history of the business. However, the company also wanted it to be interactive, so that if a visitor walked up to the screen and tapped it, more details would unfold one-by-one.

The problem? This grand plan required combining two very different concepts that rarely fold together in a quick-and-easy way: Large-scale visual storytelling combined with an intimate, personalized interactive display. As we explained to the client, a tiny pull-out display tucked inside a giant video wall undoes much of the jaw-dropping effect of the wall.

That said, we understood (and loved!) the goal, and so we set out to find a solution that would fit the client's vision while remaining functional and aesthetically impressive. Ultimately, we installed a very large, non-interactive story for the video wall, as well as smaller interactive tablets that allowed visitors to actually control the content on the video wall from afar. In doing so, we accomodated the interactivity the customer craved and created a more impactful experience for the audience.

Clients have a number of options in the journey to the perfect device. If the company has a particular brand or OS preference, that's an early factor. From there, we have conversations about what size the screen(s) ought to be. For big internal announcements and bulletins, a large video screen sends those updates loud and clear; for consumer-facing projects, the screen should likely be even higher-quality. Smaller screens work best for interactive kiosks, but there's a lot of room for exploration there.

Another question to consider is whether to go embedded or non-embedded, which determines whether the processor is part of the machine itself, running the content in real time, or is streaming content that's generated elsewhere. Non-embedded means that the processor is external to the display, like a PC or similar purpose-built device.

One of my favorite experiences with embedded processors was with a client of ours — a food service company that operates in stadiums. Those boards need to be up and running with zero downtime during events. For that reason, we opted for an embedded player that also has the ability to run a wireless signal. That means we were able to provide redundancy by using an external media player as a primary source for content playback. That way, if that device were to fail, we could easily switch the content to run on the embedded players, so there's no risk of a loss of service during concerts, games or other huge, highly-profitable events.

THE DIFFERENCES BETWEEN INTERACTIVITY AND VISUAL-ONLY

There's always a choice to make between non-interactive and interactive signage, and this is a decision where mistakes are frequently made. People are inclined to go overboard here, prioritizing what sounds cool over what will actually resonate. Interactive screens, we advise, should be used only when they serve a real purpose for customer service or audience interaction.

I'll refer here to a past client that had a massive, multi-winged office space to work with. They wanted a kiosk in the lobby that would provide an interactive map to employees and visitors to guide them through the office. Initially, the engagement was awesome! There was a real problem — people didn't know where to find certain conference rooms, offices, or even bathrooms — and many employees were quick to make use of the kiosk. The problem? After navigating on-screen, nearly the moment each person walked away, he or she completely forgot where they were going.

The lesson here is an interesting one. In some circumstances, technology actually inhibits mental mapmaking, meaning that when a user has a virtual map, he or she is less likely to retain the directions in physical reality.[5] (This is also true when we use iPhone or car GPS directions.) The follow-up solution here took some time to figure out, but we eventually opted to push the map from the kiosk to a mobile browser, allowing the user to continue following a map to their destination after walking away from the kiosk.

I like this case because I'm all about the coexistence of devices. This problem was resolved by making use of a device already conveniently located in each and every employee's pocket. We touched on this idea a bit during a conversation with one of our aforementioned partners, Sprinklr: "There's this instinct to want to make everything a touchscreen and yet nobody sees themselves as that type of shopper," VP Justin Garrity explained. "Because no one wants to use those things. Everyone's [theoretically] very excited about touchscreens, but ATMs are touchscreens, and no one's talking about them." In other words, don't let the novelty or "wow" factor overpower the genuine purpose of the tech.

KNOW YOUR LIMITATIONS BEFORE RUNNING FULL-SPEED AHEAD

Our other two criteria for device implementation are Limitation and Availability. These are demonstrated well by a popular athletic brand we've worked with. The brand wanted to install an in-store digital display that would allow customers to virtually kick a soccer ball. This requires the consumer's physical action to be monitored and transmitted on-screen.

It was, no doubt, a really great concept, and also very high-concept. As we discussed the idea in-depth, we explained that while this would be possible, it would require a custom system that a virtual reality agency would need months to create. It would cost hundreds of thousands of dollars — per store. And this was a client with a whole lot of retail locations.

As we expected, the brand understandably balked at the price and time length estimates. That's where the conversation really got interesting. We asked them, "What is the purpose of this project?" Their answer was simple: They wanted to increase engagement and make customers feel like they were truly part of the brand experience. That's an excellent answer, and one that leaves us with a lot of room for creativity.

Instead of the incredibly expensive initial blueprint, we worked together to develop a customized but relatively simple digital signage strategy that would interpret and broadcast social media posts in real time, sharing socially relevant content about the products in stores. We used data tools to analyze demographics, which allows the screens to broadcast information relevant to each customer.

The engagement numbers said it all: This system, despite being several notches less complicated than their original idea, was just as effective. The major investment costs of the VR idea would not have been justified, which the client readily acknowledged as soon as they started to see their new system in action.

In other cases, the solution to a seemingly very layered problem might just come down to less dramatic challenges in limitations and availability: An oddly shaped/limited wall space, inability to run data (in this case an embedded chip [SoC - or System-on-a-Chip] solution makes the most sense eliminating the need for an external media player and using Wi-Fi for connectivity.), and other environmental concerns are frequent thorns that can easily be resolved.

When choosing a device, if a client has a specific brand preference, we weigh in with our comprehensive knowledge and advise them about availability, cost and comparable alternatives. It's important to me that Industry Weapon is manufacturer and operating-system agnostic. That allows us to be more flexible in the types of devices we can provide and advise our clients on. And I don't feel like we need to micromanage certain decisions for our clients. You've always been loyal to Samsung? Great! You'd never consider anything not made by HP? No problem. We want to be amenable and in the know about all types of brands and devices.

Because we're primarily a software and strategy company, we don't sell clients the hardware ourselves. Instead, we typically lease hardware to clients or advise them on what to buy if they know they want to own those models. This setup not only makes financial sense for us, but it also means that we don't really have an incentive to push new hardware on clients.

That's something our clients appreciate — we're not trying to tack additional costs onto their investment. We own the hardware we lease, so if we have to replace or switch out machines, we eat that cost. That's completely fine with me. I want the team to focus on optimizing the individual strategy, and I've found that getting too attached to particular devices can get in the way.

Sometimes clients prefer to buy or lease equipment on their own, and in that case we like to do a quarterly consultation with the marketing team about what their current needs are and where they see the strategy headed in the future. If customers do want to lease the items, we have ongoing consultations in case their needs change, and then whenever necessary, we can swap out hardware accordingly.

Initiatives change over time, so this method of having periodic consultations makes a lot of sense with our business model. We do, every so often, run into some overhead costs for buying new machines, but because we're a service-based company, the expense is usually offset by the lease and the actual software and strategy service — our bread and butter.

THE AUDIENCE ENGAGEMENT FRAMEWORK™

A clearly defined structure which makes up today's most successful digital communications deployments

YOUR DEVICES MUST BE ABLE TO TELL YOUR DIGITAL STORY

PURPOSE

Focus on a device that will support the digital story you are looking to tell. The most powerful device isn't always the best fit.

AVAILABILITY

Make sure you pick a device with comparable replacement options across multiple brands to keep your deployment nimble.

LIMITATIONS

Make sure that your device can handle the physical, network and technical hurdles it faces.

A CLOSER LOOK: HOW DIGITAL INTEGRATIONS FLOPPED IN FAST-FOOD

Let's talk about to a real-world case study of the impact of sub-par digital signage integration inside a popular retail space. McDonald's, no doubt one of the world's biggest corporate success stories, recently found itself facing unexpected issues after installing digital signage and interactive kiosks into a ton of locations across the globe, eliciting results that were mixed at best.

The idea was good: Digital menu screens are more eye-catching and aesthetically pleasing than ordinary menu boards. They can be easily programmed for new promotions or off-hours brand messaging. The concept was solid. But even a seemingly foolproof idea can go wrong fast.

Not long after this initial introduction of digital menu boards, corporate messaging soon went into overdrive. Video graphics and day parting (the switching of menu items at different parts of the day, with separate breakfast, lunch, and dinner menus), confused customers. It was especially overwhelming and frustrating for older patrons who were more unfamiliar with navigating digital information.

One mistake a lot of QSR's make is that they'll move items around or overlay the entire screen with a video, which is distracting when a customer is trying to figure out what to order. It's important to respect the long-standing components of a menu board that patrons are very familiar with. For example, they expect to look at one screen for drink options and another for food. There are strategic ways to accommodate this with digital signage. For example, you can keep the drink menu in its standard location while adding a motion feature, which improves engagement without sacrificing clarity.

But McDonald's didn't foresee those early pain points and barrelled on ahead, making a bold bet that interactive order kiosks would unilaterally increase efficiency. Touch-screen order boards were installed to supplement, and in some ways replace, normal cashiers. Again, this alienated older customers, many of whom were baffled and intimidated by this process.

On the other end of the spectrum, millennial customers were dissatisfied by what they considered to be a bare-bones system. They wanted to customize their orders, and the digital platforms weren't equipped to handle those requests. Oh, and on top of all that, a study by Metro found that all touch screens tested were contaminated with fecal matter, an instance of technological advances being unable to anticipate the primitive hygiene practices of certain consumers.[6]

This is a clear case of a brand becoming invested in devices without first considering what those devices were *for*. What story did the company want to tell? What data or design choices was the brand trying to integrate? Instead of making these judgment calls first, McDonald's installed fancy-looking technology with the intention of increasing efficiency, productivity, and engagement. Instead, it alienated consumers, had a middling effect on productivity, and raised red flags for hygiene experts.

That's not to say there wasn't a good way to move forward with digital signage on these properties. We've worked with comparable food chains and higher-end restaurants and have worked out some of those difficulties that threw McDonald's for loop. Our recomendation for Mickey D's would've been to stick with more traditional-looking menu boards with the occasional, non-intrusive animation or brand videos. For hourly menu changes, we'd advise either a 24-hour selection or a clear demarcation of when, exactly, the switches occur.

If they wanted to optimize based on demographic information, we could do a pretty simple data integration there as well. Regions and ages are no small variables. While the daily clientele of a South Florida fast food chain may skew toward older people who like the standard burger and fries, it just may be that the restaurant location is just off a highly-trafficked highway. Visitors coming off that highway may, in fact, skew younger and more health-conscious. The fix? During rush hours, the franchise should maintain the existing menu while also promoting salads, yogurts and other low-calorie options. With minimal risk or heavy investment, that location is pulled right into the 21st century. By changing what's promoted but keeping the other menu items in view, the signage is guiding the audience toward its preferred (and smarter) choices while still catering to patrons who prefer the long-standing options they love.

These are lessons that aren't always obvious at face value. It's easy for us to look at the trial-and-error processes of large companies like McDonald's, and it's no deep embarrassment on their end that the integration proved rocky. It takes a lot of careful monitoring, problem-solving and spot-correcting to figure out exactly the right formula for your specific brand.

CASE STUDY: QUICKEN LOANS ARENA

One of the most successful—and impressive—uses of technology I've seen a client dream up was inside Quicken Loans Arena, the home of the Cleveland Cavaliers. Our joint project with food service brand Aramark was called "The Launch Test Kitchen." The concept: The entire look, layout and aesthetic of the kitchen could be transformed in a matter of minutes just by adjusting the digital display. Whether it's the Fourth of July, a championship game or a special private event, facility operators are able to switch everything up accordingly with just a few simple steps.

This is an instance where the **Purpose** of the project was clear from the get-go, and that intention made all the difference: Create an adaptive, immersive experience for fans. And it's not just for Cavaliers fans: Visitors entering the arena for concerts, hockey games or other special events are treated to their own customized digital signage experience. Because the devices were **Available** -- we were able to provide redundant availability using the external and embedded player scenario I mentioned before -- we seamlessly executed the purpose with our client. In fact, the technology required was mostly standard video screens and lighting; the customization came from adapting the programming to the target audience.

And while this project sounds (and looks!) ambitious, it was ultimately **Limited** in scope: We were specifically working with one enclosed area of the venue. We were careful to stick to the plan, curbing any urge to go overboard, which can derail a project. To that end, we didn't implement unnecessary touchscreens or interrupt the core customer experience of ordering food.

The project was remarkably successful, and I can't help but compare it to the less-than-ideal initial execution we talked about earlier at McDonald's. From start to finish, every element of this strategy was carefully worked out in advance with the core audience in mind.

Example of the Aramark Launch Test Kitchen dynamically changing its theme based on the event. **Photo courtesy Aramark**

CHAPTER 6

WHAT DO WE DO WITH ATTENTION ONCE WE HAVE IT?

What if you and your digital signage platform could know exactly who was in front of your sign at every second of every day? With that information at your disposal, you could put your digital signage content on autopilot, and simply broadcast the most relevant piece of content to the specific person whose eyes are on the screen. Is that something you want?

More important question: Is that something your audience wants?

Your smartphone—and all its various social media and ecommerce apps—essentially functions in this way. It analyzes what you're looking at in real time and tries to provide you with the content its algorithm determines you want to see. In other words, it's constantly re-prioritizing and customizing content, which is designed to keep you scrolling and, ideally, making purchases.

I'll explain later in this chapter why, while this technology is fascinating, it is **not** a strategy you want to employ for your digital signage—even though you very well may have the capability.

At this point, I think we've nailed down the components to effectively capturing attention: Design, integration of meaningful data, and proper device implementation are key. Now we're going to talk about how to keep your audience's attention, both in individual interactions and throughout the evolution of your digital signage strategy.

Right off the bat, we have two basic scenarios. In the first model, we have to compete with other variables to snag attention from people who are in physical motion, i.e., walking past the signage while en route to somewhere else. Those people are one-time or non-daily visitors, like a shopper who stops in a store while looking for new sneakers. Once she gets those sneakers, she's not going to be back anytime soon. In the other model, there is a captive audience in which people are static for long periods of time and essentially have no choice but to look to the signage as a source of information. An example of this is a call center, where staffers are seated at their desks for hours on end.

And in-between those two models, there's a big middle ground of consistent audiences. In an office environment, for example, employees can be classified as a type of "captive audience" since they walk through the same halls day after day. At some point, every one of those individuals is going to take a look at the digital signage. Our job is to ensure that once they take a look, they'll be intrigued enough to look again upon the next walk-by.

So, within these standard models, how do we strategize to maximize dwell time[7] in front of our screens and engagement with our strategy? We talked about it a bit earlier: Deploying personally and socially relevant information. There's a reason that people look to the information screens in airports for their flight information, even though they may have equivalent information on their phone or plane ticket. It's because that board is perceived as reliable and uniquely designed to dispense the necessary details. The audience trusts that board and will return to it with a sense of purpose.

SEEING SOCIAL RELEVANCE IN ACTION

One early learning moment for Industry Weapon was drawn from an installation we did inside a hockey rink at Robert Morris University. The plan, we thought, was well-conceived: We installed signs near high-traffic points in the facility, areas frequented by players and guests, and produced a nice blend of socially relevant content about the game and the facility. We also featured messaging about meal deals and special events going on. And yet our most important audience, the hockey players themselves, were blasting right by our screens. Dwell time was one second or less.

I was perplexed by this. The programming checked all of our boxes. Upon taking a closer look at the data results, we realized we'd overlooked one major capability of the signage: Navigation. Because we'd become so familiar with the layout of the rink, we hadn't considered that new or visiting players would be unaware of that information.

Sure, they could eventually figure out on their own which locker room to use or how to find a practice rink, but this is a pretty big facility we're talking about. Upon entering the rink, players were focused on figuring out where they were headed, so they wouldn't take the time to read extraneous messaging. After we course-corrected, adding relevant layout and directional information on top of the social programming, dwell time shot right up to those numbers we were looking for.

MAKING THE MOST OF CORPORATE COMMUNICATIONS

We talked earlier about using fun, fresh digital signage in corporate environments to keep employees engaged and improve talent retention. But even impeccable programming runs the risk of employees perceiving the screens as corporate propaganda and thus tuning it out.

One of the ways we prevent this is by switching up the format every so often, so that even if the information is roughly the same, viewers who see the screen out the corner of their eye will register the new format and perceive it as new information, at least for long enough to re-engage them.

We're not just talking about the visual format here — the delivery and wording of information should be modified so that even if the message isn't brand-new, the phrasing is. It's also important to gauge interest in features like weather updates. (We've found those are particularly engaging near parking garages. Employees really dig a traffic map that tells them how long their commute will be, whether they should consider taking an alternative route home, etc.). Where we really shake things up are emergency messages or PSAs. That's when it's time to dramatically change the color scheme and format.

73%

percent of students **did not receive** an SMS **warning** after a 2018 **armed intruder incident** at American University

Does Your Emergency Notification System Inspire Action?

Data based on a survey performed post incident by American University student, Ryan Barto revealed alarming facts about the effectiveness of their system[1].

338 students surveyed	91 received alert	247 did not receive alert

CODE RED: A FEW NOTES ON EMERGENCY MESSAGING

In an emergency situation, there is no such thing as overkill. Every last method of communication should be utilized in order to protect every last person. There's no need to wait until something happens to realize you could've been better prepared. My team has had the privilege of working with varied experts in security, from IT professionals in school districts to private corporate and home security businesses.

One of our clients, Singlewire, has impressed me at every turn with their program, which blends Industry Weapon's digital signage system with their established cell phone push notification process. Because people so often check their phones, push notifications are a vital tool during times of crisis. They can be life-saving forms of communication. However, expert studies have determined that in emergencies, pushes to cell phones only effectively notify 80% of people.

Why? Because phones are often muted, tucked away in briefcases, in an area with poor reception, left behind while a person is in the bathroom — as glued as we feel to our phones, we aren't truly attached at the hip. Further, push notifications don't go to every single person in a particular area; the cell phone owner has to specifically subscribe to them. That means visitors, clients, patients, passersby and so on will not receive critical emergency alerts. Countless people potentially at risk may not be within your organization's network.

You only have to look at the spike in bulletproof backpack sales to see that students are rightfully concerned about unforeseen dire circumstances on campus. American University students expressed shock and concern in 2018 when failures in the school's emergency alert system seemingly put them in danger during a lockdown situation. Months later, in spring 2019, many University of Michigan students shared their discontentment and panic after receiving a poorly-phrased "active shooter" alert that turned out to be a false alarm. It's absolutely critical that people have immediate access to clear, updated, relevant information during emergencies.

In legitimate code-red situations, our client's program makes it impossible for people to ignore or discount word of a pressing issue. When people get a text notification while the overhead speaker is blaring, their computers are suddenly flashing, the phones are broadcasting, digital signage displays are scrolling text — nobody is going to ignore that. They're going to respond accordingly.

ACQUAINT YOURSELF WITH THESE ACRONYMS: KPIS, SLA AND SELS

For more captive audiences, our standards are slightly different. The digital signage in call or sales centers are generally very purpose-based; we might have occasional change-ups in our messaging, but generally we want a pretty constant stream of up-to-date KPI's to make sure we're in keeping with our Service Level Agreement, or SLA. For example, if the average call time is one minute and thirty seconds, we're going to want to post that so staffers have a performance benchmark and firm understanding of how they should be operating to remain competitive. This is particularly important for brands who adhere to a tight time promise for consumers. Most marketing professionals call this "gamification," although I prefer the term "friendly competition."

This is the same principle we talked about earlier with AngioDynamics, where KPIs were posted on digital signage throughout the manufacturing floor, keeping workers abreast of performance for the day. If the team is falling below the service level agreement or there's another gap in performance at the call center, the digital signage can respond accordingly, re-formatting or re-coloring the content in order to instantly get that information across.

Let's talk a bit more about SEL: Simple Exclusive Limited Time Offers. These types of offers can bump up engagement with customers who are already in your store, and motivate them to return again in the near future in the hopes of snagging another great deal.

Consider, for example, the old K-mart "blue light specials." After abandoning them for quite some time, the brand recently brought them back in hopes of boosting flagging performance. If you never experienced a blue light special during their initial run, it was quite an experience! Out of nowhere, a loudspeaker would announce "ATTENTION KMART SHOPPERS" and blue lights would go off to announce a sudden deal: "For the next thirty minutes, jeans are 50% off!" Cue the mad rush to the denim shelves.

Not only did this setup encourage sales and dwell time in that moment, but it also motivated customers to return for similar deals at a later date. Other retailers have also seen the value in offering special off-peak hour deals, which can drive significant additional sales. These are venerable sales strategies, but when you couple them with modern technology, they can be a force to be reckoned with. SEL is a great technique that encourages consumer interaction and engagement before the installation of interactive kiosks, which take programming to a whole new level.

ECOMMERCE HAS CHANGED THE WAY RETAILERS PROVIDE EXCLUSIVE SHOPPING EXPERIENCES.

PERSONALIZED ENGAGEMENT

Social engagement analytics provide retailers with unprecedented insights products the customer wants with simple ways to re-target and serve up related content they care about.

TIME SENSITIVE OFFERS

The scarcity of real time inventory and live countdowns create a real-time sense of urgency. When the timer runs out, the product is really gone and consumers are now wired to react.

HYPER-TARGETED OFFERS

Customer shopping habits, past orders and buyer personas allow retailers to target customers and deliver exclusive offers with precision accuracy.

BUT HOW DO YOU CREATE THESE EXPERIENCES IN BRICK & MORTAR?

SIMPLE
The offer can be understood in less than 6 seconds.

EXCLUSIVE
Localizing the offer creates a boutique style experience for even the largest retailer.

LIMITED OFFERS
Clearly demonstrate scarcity of the offer based on product availability, time or both.

SEL Uses Digital Signage to Create Dynamic Shopping Experiences.

SIMPLE — Content is to-the-point and can be understood in several seconds

LIMITED OFFER — Offers expire after brief period of time

EXCLUSIVE — Offers are unique to individual store locations

THERE IS EVIDENCE THAT EFFECTIVE USE OF DIGITAL SIGNAGE WILL BOOST SALES OF ITEMS THAT ARE NOT SELLING WELL BY 10%, WHILE IMPULSE PURCHASING CAN BE INCREASED UP TO 20%

USING DATA TO BOOST SALES WITHOUT BECOMING BIG BROTHER

Should digital signage operate like a smartphone? In other words, if you have the capability to determine in real-time just who is looking at your programming, should the message auto-customize to directly relate to that person? It's doable: Many of our signs have cameras in them, and software installations can determine demographic variables like age, sex and race. We know that successful marketing typically caters heavily to its intended audience, using these types of parameters, so why not incorporate this information into our digital signage strategies?

I'll tell you exactly why. Most people, myself included, find that instantaneous updates based on demographic information is pretty disturbing and invasive. That means that even if you get the message exactly right, you're running a high risk of creeping out your audience instead of appealing to them.

Just in the last few years, the general public has become remarkably attuned to data-driven advertising. Everybody notices — and is freaked out — when a conversation about "dog food" magically leads to Facebook ads for dog food. It's obvious, and people don't like it. It's a big reason why many companies, Facebook included, have lost public trust and have made little gains to reclaim it.

That said, building a general profile — one that feels useful and relevant, not hyper-specific and alarming — certainly can be useful on both the brand and audience ends. That's why we aim to strike the perfect balance. To completely disregard the capabilities of smart data would be unwise given how genuinely beneficial it can be to the parties involved.

Here's an example that won't keep you up at night, wondering if corporate America is spying on you: If most of the people viewing a digital sign at 10 AM on Wednesdays are women 35 years and older, there's no harm in optimizing for that overarching demographic. But if a 17-year-old male suddenly wanders into the vicinity, we're not going to suddenly abandon the programming for something customized for him. That would be extremely noticeable and distressing. By using data wisely, we can evaluate trends and respond accordingly, maximizing impact without causing a scene.

HOW DATA AND SOCIAL INTEGRATIONS CAN IMPACT BUSINESS

I always enjoy talking with other digital media leaders across the industry to broaden my own understanding of this ever-changing field. We had a great Business Impact Workshop chat with Sprinklr. They're constantly monitoring these solutions, deploying the software and making adjustments as needed until the final product is smarter, sleeker and stronger. It's not about repeatedly starting from scratch; rather, it's about improving on already-awesome product. "You can retain your [existing] creative but also put in content that's more dynamic," VP Justin Garrity explained. These designs "change every day or once a week, making it really interesting to look at."

One program that's already transforming the marketing industry is a system that combs through social media to gauge consumer commentary. As people start buzzing about a new product online, the program tracks those responses. That real-world feedback enables the program to determine what's really resonating with customers — vital information for the company's marketing team. As Garrity put it: Let's say you have a new product in five colors. Before you roll out that product, you have to create marketing materials to display in the store. One color is going to have to take center stage, but it's impossible to predict which one is going to be the biggest hit with shoppers.

And once those sales numbers do come in months later, the products are no longer brand-new, and there's not much incentive to create all-new marketing materials.

"Just like marketing teams have gotten used to doing variants for email ads, we are encouraging brands to do variants for in-store creative," he said. "Use our listening platform to listen to social conversations in real-time, and apply positive sentiment analysis" to modify existing creative for the most successful long-term impact.

Social analytics are just the beginning. More and more programs in development will help boost the impact of digital signage, creating a customized experience that feels personal and relevant for the target audience.

A FAVORITE INTERNAL STRATEGY IS TO USE OUR VOICE

VOICE is our acronym for "Verifiable Open Information for Consumer Enlightenment." It's mostly specific to retail and is designed to mimic the strategy that many brands successfully use with e-commerce: Leveraging user-generated and influencer-generated social media content to help drive the customer's decision to make a purchase.

The stats are big: Seventy percent of brands use influencer content as part of their marketing strategy, and ninety percent of US consumers say user-generated content has the biggest impact on their purchase decisions. In other words, the potential here is massive -- and yet it's strangely overlooked by most brick-and-mortar retail locations.

We touched briefly on this in Chapter 4 when we discussed integrating social media into your retail strategy or into your corporate communications. This kind of information feels like it comes from a trustworthy but objective third party. With VOICE, we bring that user-generated and influencer-generated content right into brick-and-mortar stores. This is a strategy that most brands, even very Gen-Z friendly ones, aren't doing today, and that's a major misstep. By marrying the Instagram, Twitter and user-generated content with core brand assets on screens in stores, we help consumers to correlate people they trust with the brand at the point of sale. There are few marketing concepts more powerful in a real-world, real-time environment.

Here's an example. If you read a product review written by a casual acquaintance who lives a few streets away, you know that review is coming from a verifiable source. You can trust that it's going to be pretty honest, and you'll value that opinion more than a slick branded ad for the product on a TV commercial. This ties right back to that crucial 70/30 split between socially relevant content and core brand messaging is essential here.

Many brands are leveraging social media chatter and user-generated content online, but few have made the jump to featuring those items in their live retail strategies. If you don't offer someone a unique, amplified experience in-store, then they have no reason not to buy online. This is the problem that VOICE and SEL help to solve.

Much of the same criteria within VOICE can be applied to our corporate communications model, although the "open information" part of the strategy may be somewhat redundant: Presumably, you're already sharing your best, most up-to-date information with your own team. Any "external" information is going to take the form of additional social media feeds, traffic cams, and weather reports. When we leverage that type of content, our clients see much higher dwell time and overall engagement.

The Solution

CORE BRAND ASSETS

Your existing in-store display materials define the guest experience.

V erified
O pen
I nsight for
C onsumer
E nlightenment

Combining brand with user generated content adds authenticity to your brand while creating personally relevant guest experiences.

USER & INFLUENCER GENERATED INSIGHTS

Content from people your customer trusts compliments the branded content experience.

Using digital signage displays, retailers have the opportunity to connect their core brand messaging with user generated/influencer content. Our simple platform allows marketers to curate unique experiences

ONE.
MORE.
MILE.

@WatchKatieRun

CONCEPT IN ACTION

Columbia Sportswear use the VOICE model to enhance their PFG Store experience. The combination of product and lifestyle content with live social media content adds relevance and true social proof to the audience in the store.

KEY TERMS:

Dwell Time: The time a viewer spends in front of digital signage. Generally, a longer dwell time is better, but the actual length of time can vary widely given the purpose and placement of the device. For digital signs in call centers, for example, you may be getting very quick but very consistently spaced glances up at your sign for KPI's, whereas in a corporate office interactions may generally only be long enough for one round of assets (< 8 seconds) or may last several minutes. For interactive kiosks, dwell time is typically longer, though interactions are less frequent.

VOICE (Verifiable Open Information for Consumer Enlightenment): This refers to items like reviews, social media posts, and other brand-relevant feeds that can be relayed through your digital signage strategy. Honesty and transparency are key.

SEL (Simple Exclusive Limited Time Offers): A marketing technique mostly exclusive to retail and hospitality, although there is certainly room for creative crossover into the corporate/internal messaging space. These offers boost sales within the window that they're active, and they also increase overall engagement with the establishment and encourage consumers to come back for more.

KPI (Key Performance Indicator): Refers to key points of data typically used to measure performance.

SLA (Service Level Agreement): The level at which service is agreed to stay for customers, generally used for call centers, and other customer-service based industries.

KEY TAKEAWAYS

+ **Purpose:** This is the most important priority when considering what devices to implement in your business. Without a clear story to tell and purpose in mind, adding technological devices can hinder performance rather than improve it.

+ **Availability:** The range of technical options for digital signage broadcasting is large, but it's important to always have a backup option in case of supply shortages, discontinuations, or an unexpected change in brand preference.

+ **Limitations:** Knowing what certain limitations are in the space at hand, whether these are architectural, data related, or even having to do with the expense of a client's ideas, is essential to good device implementation.

+ **Device Options:** These include size, touchscreen vs non-interactive and embedded vs non-embedded chips.

CHAPTER 7

CREATIVELY ADAPTING TO A CHANGING LANDSCAPE

Scary question: How does a once-dominant retail giant go bankrupt?

The most obvious response is "poor investments." Could be the case, but it's often not; even financially risk-averse companies can find themselves belly-up. There's another variable at play, and it takes no prisoners: E-commerce.

Every single person retail is attempting to calmly navigate the beast that is e-commerce. Amazon is gobbling up many retailers, or at least shrinking their reach, and businesses are struggling to adapt their online and in-store strategies. Retailers spend so much time worrying about remaining competitive online that they're overwhelmingly at a loss in regards to strategizing within their own physical stores. They scramble to hire consultants and marketing gurus to optimize their online strategies and leave their retail stores to fend for themselves.

Here's a quick example from a recent shopping trip of my own. All I needed were plain white shoelaces to replace my grayed ones, and I was in New York City — an American mecca of shopping. I was in Union Square, a tourist-heavy region flooded with eager shoppers and dozens of stores. So you can imagine my frustration and irritation when, as I entered no fewer than five different stores,

I was informed that there were no white shoelaces on hand. A department store, a branded shoe place, an athletics store: None of them had flat white laces for my sneakers. And, of course, I found myself having the thought that plagues brick-and-mortar retailers across the globe: "I should've just ordered them online."

In case you're on the edge of your seat, I'll fill you in on the conclusion. Despite an employee of one of the stores telling me "I don't think we carry shoelaces," I managed to find a package in that very location, albeit in a strange spot. (Keep 'em near the shoes!) Imagine how much less of a nightmare it would've been if I could have tapped an interactive kiosk to see a comprehensive store map that directed me toward exactly what I needed.

Websites are less exhausting to navigate than big stores, but that doesn't mean they're necessarily preferable shopping experiences. We've found that by adapting many of the practices from online to physical retail stores (and the digital signage strategies within), retailers are able to see significant improvements in consumer engagement and sales in-store.

One great example of this concept in action is Social Media Marketing. It's heavily utilized by e-commerce outlets but can also work exceptionally well when cast on in-store digital signage. Recall our work with Finish Line (a store that does, to its credit, carry plenty of shoelaces): Customers were able to view social media buzz about the shoes they were interested in, as they would online, with the added bonus of *physically handling* the shoes in order to get the information, thus forming a stronger psychological bond with the product. This coupled with the fact that our display was specially organized and curated, with a gorgeous high-resolution screen, achieving a far greater impact than a consumer would have with a phone screen or laptop.

I asked above how a retail giant could crash and burn. I'm thinking of one in particular, and its cardinal sin was a failure to adapt and innovate. It's Sears, which had one of the most revolutionary marketing schemes of the 20th century, the Sears catalogue, and was ironically unable to keep up with the changes brought by the 21st century and ecommerce. Ironic because, in many ways, Amazon is itself essentially a brilliantly optimized online catalogue. Because Sears couldn't make the jump to online, their store which had once been at the forefront of retail strategy became a fossil. That's in contrast to how how a flagging Kmart brought back the "Blue Light" sales like we discussed earlier.

The frontier of retail strategy is all about making the physical store a special event, more than the simple transaction you get online. Of course the ultimate goal is to make the sale, but by building your brand in this physical space, you can do so in a much more meaningful way than with an online banner ad, and see engaged, repeat customers as a result.

HOW ONE OF OUR CLIENTS IS FIGHTING THE RETAIL BATTLE WITH DIGITAL SIGNAGE

The sporting goods retailer Orvis has taken this strategy and run with it. "It's not a battle to me between retail and digital; it's a blending of how they're used," said Dave Finnegan, CXO. He encourages what he calls the "omni experience" in his stores by combining the best of both worlds in digital and physical stores. During our Business Impact Workshop with Dave, he emphasized how in physical stores people will touch the objects in store (a concept we talked about a few pages back in regards to Finish Line). When you combine the benefits of digital media and the customer physically being there, you achieve a powerful connection with your product, and a profound in-store experience.

Dave's team doesn't stop at high-level theory. He and the rest of the Orvis team like to "work backwards" from common marketing problems and develop solutions from there. For example, when it came time to approach the always-difficult holiday of Father's Day, out-of-the-box thinking led to excellent strategy. A bit of thoughtful reflection and analysis led the team to realize that dads are hard to shop for because they're not nearly as interested in physical gifts as they are in spending quality time with their kids. In other words: A key set of intangibles. From there, Orvis worked to develop a marketing plan that would make the connection between these intangibles and their store's actual products.

Dave's team also takes a page out of Industry Weapon's data playbook: rather than reviewing numbers quarterly, his company reviews gross profit every day in order to keep up-to-date on their performance and adapt to problems or pain points as they come up. This culminates in an end-of-the-year "playback" performance review where the company reviews as a whole what has worked for them and what hasn't. While it may sound intimidating, the utter openness with which they handle their performance data actually fosters increased trust and performance among team members.

"Our team's scorecards for marketing and merchandising are gross profit based," Dave said. "We know what our gross profit is every day — we don't have to wait until the end of the month to see how we did."

Incorporating digital elements into their stores has helped Orvis to really take its brand to the next level. When you walk into any Orvis location, you're going to get, as Dave calls it, the omni experience: Passionate employees who are knowledgeable about the products, digital signage that helps customers determine what exactly they're looking for, and top-tier products they'll want to bring home that day.

DIGITAL SIGNAGE IN THE K-12 SPACE

One of our most creative clients is, believe it or not, the Mobile County public school system. You might think that public schooling is pretty far from retail, but we actually see that some of the same strategies of engagement and audience participation actually work very well in a public school setting.

While many public school systems have some kind of digital signage strategy in place, we've helped them to implement a more responsive, visually compelling, and socially relevant program than almost any other school district. Furthermore, Mobile has managed to leverage public spaces into "incidental learning areas," much like the transitional spaces we talked about in our first chapter. In lunchrooms, they've run a quiz game between lunch tables on key curriculum subjects. The school actually saw a significant increase in test scores on that subject.

On a separate but related note, the Mobile Public School systems also implemented a reactive colored lighting system to improve school safety. During an emergency like a fire or active shooter situation, hallways will be light either green or red in response to the emergency. Green hallways are safe to go down, while red hallways are not. It's a unique way that the school has utilized analog technology (hallway lighting) in tandem with the new digital systems.

The same school has also implemented responsive lighting, which adjusts its brightness based on the amount of ambient light coming in from outside. This increased energy efficiency and academic performance, as the harsh fluorescent lighting normally used in public schools has been shown to negatively impact focus and cause eye strain. Let's go a bit more in-depth.

IT'S LONG PAST TIME TO MAKE SAFETY A PRIORITY

Keeping kids both safe and engaged inside school buildings is a perpetual challenge, and it's only worsened in recent years as technology has become more personal. When an important message needs to be received, like an emergency alert or an unexpected announcement, it's non-negotiable that the kids need to get that information.

We were really excited to team up with Mobile County to tackle this, and what made it even more enjoyable was that the district's Chief Information Officer, David Akridge, already had some stellar ideas in the works.

Picture one of your high school classrooms. Or better yet, the cafeteria. Remember those long beams of blue-gray light — the ones that made everyone look a little bit sick? Turns out, the research says it all: Fluorescent lighting makes for an awful working environment, inducing major eye strain for students, reducing productivity and overall reducing the pleasantry of a building where students and staff spend the majority of their lives.

The solution inside Mobile County? Digital lighting. "It allows the optimal type of lighting to be in the room — it fluctuates throughout the day as the light changes outside," Akridge explained as we met with him to talk digital integrations in K-12 school facilities. It's had, he said, a "tremendous effect' — and not just for students. It's also a cost-effective solution for after-hours: "As a security guard walks through the building at 9:00 at night, the lights come on as he's walking and turn off as he passes. I don't have to leave the lights on 24/7."

From there, Akridge kept thinking. How else could the school utilize lighting to resolve issues? The idea came to him after he borrowed a set of beacon lights, which allow the user to mix color combinations, for his daughter's wedding. What if the school employed colored lighting to signify emergency situations, like a visual alarm? The idea made total sense, but the product — something branded as an emergency lighting system for schools — wasn't on the market. No one else had thought of it.

He thought, "Someone can make this lighting system." So he started making calls. "We called a company and told them, and they said nobody's ever needed it, but we can do it."

Think about it. It's so simple, and it's brilliant: Everyone's thinking about digital displays, intercom systems, automated text alerts. But lighting is universal. You walk down the hall, the lights suddenly turn red, and just about every last student instantly knows what it means. At Industry Weapon, we love ideas like this. We start with an awesome idea like Akridge's, and we build on it, using digital signage to amp up the impact and make the system more effective and impactful.

USING TECH TO STIMULATE APATHETIC STUDENTS

Whew. This is one of those problems that schools have always had. Some people just aren't naturally great students — they don't like to sit in class, they have trouble focusing, they quickly become bored or frustrated or straight-up angry. According to Akridge, the issue has only gotten worse over time as kids become less and less convinced that getting an education is fundamental.

"Kids today ... would just as soon fail school if they don't see a necessity for it," he said. "So many of our kids are checked out because they're just not engaged."

Technology is finally helping staff develop solutions to the perennial issue of the apathetic student. The general idea? Even if there's just one class a student adores — for example, video production — that student will show up for school each day, even if it's just in anticipation of using state-of-the-art equipment to pursue their passions.

There's that famous quote "If you do what you love, you'll never work a day in your life." We often don't start encouraging that mindset until college or even years into a career. High school isn't a throwaway four years; it really does set the stage for the rest of a person's life.

Digital signage helps faculty to better convey to students just how many opportunities are at their fingertips. When designed appropriately, the messaging catches students' eyes and piques interest, ideally encouraging them to try out for that comedy troupe or attend an after-school graphic design club gathering.

CHANGE IS GOOD, KID

There are a lot of reasons why people fear change, in and out of their work lives. The idea of the unknown can be, quite frankly, terrifying. And change is antithetical to stability, which is what most people are looking for in their jobs: They want to feel confident that their jobs are secure.

Technology intimidates people in the workplace because, on some level, they're afraid that they — as less-than-perfect humans — will become obsolete. They also worry that incorporating technology implies that they're not doing their jobs as well as possible. And many people are concerned that they won't be able to fully understand how to use new tools.

We were genuinely surprised to realize that so many schools look and operate exactly as they did 30 (or more) years ago. But it makes sense: Teachers learned how to teach a certain way, and they're often resistant to change, especially when they feel their methods have always worked just fine.

During a video conference with Cisco and dozens of other school districts, the schools were asked what hindrances get in their way as they try to modernize their buildings. The answer was overwhelming, nearly unanimous. "Tradition and lack of wanting to change," Akridge said. "People just don't want to change."

In other words, people who were in high school decades ago don't understand why things should run any differently today than they did back then. It's a theme that's certainly not limited to the education sector. Akridge told us that during a conference with Microsoft, more than three-quarters of companies from all types of industries reported that their own employees were resistant to technological change in the workplace: "It's not the technology that's the problem," he said. "It's not the things we're coming up with. It's trying to overcome the fear factory, the complacency and comfort."

We took a tour through Mobile's school buildings and while there was new technology folded into the infrastructure, it certainly wasn't overwhelming or distracting. Teachers adjust and thrive, even if there's a period of transition as they get used to new tools, like digital smart boards instead of chalkboards.

Perhaps part of the fear is that employees worry they'll ultimately be replaced by technology. It's a fear with which many people, especially those of older generations, struggle. But the fact is, even as we bring technology into schools, teachers remain crucial. Indispensable. Students still need skilled, dedicated teachers, and new tools simply help those teachers do their jobs as effectively as possible. "Change is hard, but we live in a society of change," Akridge said. "And the kids are demanding it."

Once you've identified a sense of employee hesitation (or full-on combat) to technological advances within the company, take some time to think carefully about the root. What are they afraid of? How can you assure your employees that their fears will be addressed and resolved?

It's important for employees to understand that their roles are not going to be diminished with the incorporation of new tech products and systems. The intention is to enhance — to make their jobs easier, to make their results bigger and better. Akridge saw that many of his district's teachers had been teaching the exact same lesson plan in their exact same way for years upon years. They resented the idea that adding new equipment to the classroom could fix something that, in their opinions, simply wasn't broken.

This is largely a symptom of generational divide. Older employees may not totally recognize that Gen Z relies heavily on tech in order to learn. The internet is not, contrary to many parents' and teachers' beliefs, a crutch. It is a new medium by which people, especially those who have grown up on it, come to understand the world.

To use Akridge's words, the students are "demanding" that their schools at least try to keep up with the fast-changing times. That's not because they're entitled. It's because this is the world they know, and this is how they study, learn and grow. That doesn't mean that books or worksheets are obsolete. It just means that the classroom should be supplemented with certain digital tools that serve the ultimate purpose of best teaching important material to students.

We took a tour through one of Mobile County's schools, and the tech integrations spoke for themselves. They help teachers teach. They help students learn. They aren't flashy or even particularly noticeable. For example, many of the classrooms are now equipped with smart boards, which are essentially digitally-enhanced chalkboards.

They have advanced functions that help the teacher demonstrate concepts much better than traditional chalk-drawn diagrams ever could. And more functionality means that students of all different learning levels will be able to follow along in ways that work for them.

Unless you work among people who are all technologically savvy, you should expect a level of resistance to change. Understand that this pushback comes out of fear, which is a powerful emotion. But with detailed explanations and comprehensive training, your employees will ultimately feel comfortable and confident as they begin incorporating tech into their work lives.

INFLUENCERS ARE HAVING A MOMENT...

While beauty and fashion brands understandably dominate Instagram — the app is ideal for beautifully spotlighting makeup, hair, clothing and the like — the photo-focused platform has become a must-have across all industries. From hospitals to daycares to auction houses, all types of businesses are utilizing Instagram to showcase their products and company culture. There's a lot of room for creativity, and when really optimized, the results can be big.

Many brands are intrigued by the idea of partnering with influencers. The influencer landscape is booming, but tread carefully: There's no shortage of social media users looking to make a quick buck by partnering with a brand. Leveraging influencers can be powerful, but there's a strategy to doing it the right way, and if you're too idealistic, you'll find yourself pouring money down the drain on a short-sighted marketing plan.

Our client Deka Lash is a quickly-expanding eyelash extension brand that owes much of their traction to social media. It's no secret that Instagram, Facebook, Twitter and the like are critical components to a successful brand in 2019 — but understanding how to actually use these platforms effectively isn't quite so simple. They've impressively navigated the world of influencers, selecting strong partners in the social media space to boost brand awareness and sales.

Let's get into it: Your product has already developed an enthusiastic fanbase. Congrats! The next step is carefully identifying which of those fans are influencers who can help you attract even more excited customers. Greg Forsyth, Deka Lash's senior director of innovation and brand strategy, was up for the challenge.

The best influencers, he explained, are already in your database. They're vocal fans of the product who purchase it — repeatedly. Most companies make the tempting but fruitless mistake of looking outside their existing clientele for potential influencers. That's a tedious process: You're combing through photos, hashtags, tweets, and, perhaps most frustratingly, devoted customers of competitors. After identifying these people, who are currently total strangers to your brand, all of the weight falls on you to convert them into genuine ambassadors.

The key word there is "genuine." Forsyth learned from his own daughter that Gen Z has a particular love for YouTubers, who become popular by showcasing their own personalities, interests and favorites. It's extremely transparent and obvious to their viewers when they attempt to sell products that they don't truly care about. When influencers are just out to make a buck by shilling random products, the dishonesty isn't lost on their audience, even those who are very young.

"You really want to be genuine, and that's where influencers have the most impact — when it's from the heart, and it doesn't sound like something a boardroom wrote for them to speak," he said. "They're talking about how much they love it and how much they use it — 'I use this product every day' — and they can mean it."

...BUT USE THEM WISELY.

Like I said, a lot of people are eager to profit off the social media space, and a quick online transaction can immediately create the appearance of a powerful influencer: They buy followers and likes, artificially inflating their prominence. Unfortunately, a surprising number of companies don't realize they're being duped.

If you take a scroll through Instagram, you'll come across dozens of accounts with thousands of followers and likes — but when you look closer look, you'll see that legitimate engagement isn't there. It's possible to fake engagement, but anyone with social media savvy will be able to see through bot-type comments.

Engagement — real engagement, not just the relatively convincing appearance of it — is critical if you want to see real-life results.

"Referral is still the #1 source of marketing — word of mouth," he said. "[Social media] is really our best way to solicit that. You can hand out coupons ... but the new way of building that word of mouth, referral, is through influencers."

So how can you separate the fakers from the real power players? A little bit of common sense can go a long way. Don't be fooled by the numbers. Take a real look at the people who are commenting and liking each post. Are they local to the area? Are they of the same age range? Are they writing personal comments that clearly show some sort of friendship? These are all indicators that an influencer is legit.

Deka Lash found that when pairing up with an influencer on Instagram, the best thing to do is just get out of the way and let him or her do their thing. Popular influencers have an unbelievable understanding of what works on the app. They know how to frame photos and write captions that engage their followers — and, ultimately, convince those followers to take an interest in your product.

That all said, influencers are only part of the equation when it comes to optimizing your Instagram presence. Take some time to get to know all the features of the app. Did you know you can livestream, showing your followers in real-time how your product works? How about the Story feature — do you know you can run polls and Q&As to really peak customer interest?

Using VOICE and SEL as a foundation for creativity

We've already covered VOICE and SEL in detail, but I want to emphasize them again for a slightly different reason: They're great examples of marketing strategies that don't require a huge degree of "creativity" while still managing to help you wind up creating strong brand culture all the same. VOICE leverages the social media posts that consumers are already making to create an interactive, authentic environment for your customers when they enter your store. A verified review from a real member of your community, cast up on a screen in-store, means a lot more to shoppers than some anonymous reviewer on Amazon.

SEL, meanwhile, takes tried-and-true sales techniques and updates them for the twenty-first century. Think interactive kiosks that know who you are and what you like, or store infrastructures that identify key traffic hours and roll out special deals optimized to increase sales and keep customers coming back. Innovative ideas are everywhere! You just have to be adaptive and dedicated to figuring out what sticks.

CLOSING THOUGHTS

The last twelve years of my life have outdone every last expectation I envisioned when Industry Weapon was in its earliest stages -- and even at the time, my expectations were already pretty lofty. When we began, it was all about providing a digital signage experience to customers to serve aesthetic or luxury purposes. Today, digital signage is *the* standard to effectively communicate with the masses.

We've brought clarity to an issue that many brands and organizations couldn't quite figure out: How do I use a digital signage software to control video walls, kiosks and digital signs? Now, that question is all but irrelevant. We're able to answer it on day one and move on to much cooler, grander, out-of-the-box goals.

Every day, my day takes stock of the biggest challenges facing businesses across all industries, and we solve those challenges by inspiring action through communication. A lot of people mistakenly think that the smartphone is the be-all, end-all of modern communication. It's just not true. It's way too busy, too crowded, to function as a targeted communication tool. There's no doubt about it: We've got to use broadcast digital media, digital signage, video walls and kiosks. They are the attention-grabbers, the message-deliverers, the mediums that make people stop and consider and buy.

The ever-present but always fun reality of working in tech is that even when we make major progress, there's always more to do, new ways to make things better. We also continue to condense the time it takes to inspire that action by making changes faster than we're able to do today. As devices continue to evolve, processor speeds continue to get better -- and the digital stories we tell we become more relevant, entertaining and purposeful.

Some things won't change. We always have to focus first on the audience and think seriously about how to truly gain and retain their attention. How to have fun and be playful. We've got to inspire action for consumers and employees. We strive to have a bigger impact on your entity's growth, but we're also in the business of helping to save lives and deliver crucial intel when it matters most -- to have real-time impact during unfolding emergencies so that we can help people get to where they need to be.

As we build our communication strategies into the future and as we see new technologies come on board, our ability to adopt and integrate with those will be mission critical. Effective broadcast digital communication will always be an emerging technology, and while we have cracked today's code for gaining audience attention, we're always working to ensure that we'll be ahead of the game for whatever tomorrow brings.

I'm excited. I'm excited to be a part of an industry that requires constant innovation and creativity from hardware, software, security and content. I'm excited to be a part of this movement, and I absolutely am excited to continue to create models and frameworks that help inspire people to take action.

Endnotes:

1 Attention Spans: https://www.scribd.com/document/265348695/Microsoft-Attention-Spans-Research-Report

2 "The Myth of Multitasking"

3 "Skim Reading is the New Normal"

4 Hierarchy and Mind Motion in Advertising Design: https://www.theartsjournal.org/index.php/site/article/view/78/77

5 Smartphones and the Uncertain Future of "Spatial Thinking": https://www.citylab.com/life/2014/09/smartphones-and-the-uncertain-future-of-spatial-thinking/379796/

6 Poo Found on Every McDonald's Touchscreen Tested: https://metro.co.uk/2018/11/28/poo-found-on-every-mcdonalds-touchscreen-tested-8178486/

7 "Dwell time" is the industry term for the time a viewer spends engaging with a digital screen

8 "We could have died." After campus lockdown, students speaks out on AU alert system: https://www.theeagleonline.com/article/2018/07/we-could-have-died-after-campus-lockdown-students-speak-out-on-au-alert-system

9 Struggling Retailer Kmart Turns the Blue Light Back On: https://www.reuters.com/article/us-kmart-bluelight/struggling-retailer-kmart-turns-the-blue-light-back-on-idUSKCN0SQ1NL20151101

DIGITAL SIGNAGE BUYERS GUIDE

 HARDWARE SOFTWARE SECURITY CONTENT

Learn the most **important questions** you should ask your provider **before investing** in a digital signage solution.

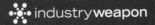 industry**weapon**

There are over 350 digital signage CMS providers in the industry today. With this amount to choose from, it's difficult to determine the best option. We've broken down the key questions you should be asking when researching a digital signage provider.

THE RISK ASSESSMENT QUADRANT

HARDWARE

Displays, media players and networking equipment in place to ensure optimal delivery of the digital story.

SOFTWARE

Management, scheduling and distribution are as hands off as possible for the IT Department

SECURITY

Your provider has your best interests in mind, securing your data and ensuring minimal impact on your network.

CONTENT

Your content team is equipped with best of breed content feeds and applications to ensure their success.

HARDWARE

Hardware includes the displays, media players, and networking equipment required to ensure optimal delivery of the digital content. Some digital signage software solutions work with very specific hardware, which may or may not be compatible with your existing infrastructure. Make sure you won't be limited to an outdated operating system or forced to pay a premium fee to upgrade to the compatible hardware needed.

WILL IT HANDLE MY NEEDS?

Existing vs. New

How can the provider support your existing hardware deployment? Does the provider offer a robust library of supported devices for a variety of use-cases operating systems and form factors?

WHY SHOULD I CARE?

Costs to rip out the old and replace with the new are the most obvious reason here. Choosing a provider who can support your existing infrastructure, even if only temporarily, will drastically reduce the impact of transitioning CMS providers.

Manufacturer Preferences

Does the provider offer flexibility to support your preferred hardware manufacturer(s)?

WHY SHOULD I CARE?

Corporate purchasing departments, especially in the enterprise, have their preferred vendors for pricing and consistency. The ability to fit your digital signage hardware into the mix makes purchasing, service and support much easier.

Mixed Deployment Capability

Does the provider support multiple operating systems, with capabilities to manage not just digital signs, but also interactive and video wall situations?

WHY SHOULD I CARE?

Your hardware needs will vary based on the content story you are looking to tell. At times, the go-to piece of hardware for 90% of your deployment will not be powerful enough or feature-rich enough to support a particular use-case. High resolution video walls and interactive displays are great examples for this. Make sure you aren't handcuffed by a particular capability or resolution.

SOFTWARE

The best digital signage software, or Content Management Solution (CMS), should do one thing above all else: deliver content to your screen. This should be simple to instigate from a user standpoint. The additional functionality is what sets providers apart. Make sure you don't pay for functionality that is broken or irrelevant to your needs.

IS IT EASY TO MANAGE?

 1

Simplicity

Does the software interface provide similar functionality to the software suites that Marketing & Communications teams are currently using?

WHY SHOULD I CARE?

Many providers base their interface on video editing tools or limit layouts to rigid templates with playlist hierarchies. The typical digital signage user - (Marketing and Communications roles), is very comfortable with apps like Photoshop and Powerpoint and expect their digital signage software interface to function similarly.

2

Training

Does the provider tie you up in paid training packages or expensive on-site workshops? Or, do they guarantee free, unlimited, one-on-one training as part of your package?

WHY SHOULD I CARE?

What comes easy to some may not be as simple to all of your users. Make sure your provider offers multiple learning channels. The best providers will not limit or charge you for one-on-one training, group sessions or quick calls just to ask a question.

3

Support

Does your provider offer free, unlimited 24/7 phone and email support? Or are you tied to paid programs to avoid email only, 24-48 hour response times?

WHY SHOULD I CARE?

Digital signage deployments are high visibility and when there are problems, you need help right away. Make sure the provider doesn't charge you to call when an issue does arise and ask about any time of day restrictions with their help desk. Don't be hung out to dry after hours or if you are in a time zone different from your CMS provider.

SECURITY

IT professionals have a ton of responsibility between staying up-to-date with the latest security protocols, and making sure each new technology purchase will benefit the organization. Your provider should invest rigorous measures to keep your data secure and minimally impact your network.

HARDWARE	SOFTWARE
SECURITY	CONTENT

SAFE FOR MY NETWORK?

SOC 2, PCI, Vulnerability Testing

What level of caution does the provider take to ensure security of your data in its data centers, code and throughout its day-to-day operations?

WHY SHOULD I CARE?

Many SaaS based content management systems will hide behind their collocation's certifications. This means that their data center itself may be audited but that doesn't speak for the software provider and how they handle your data within their offices. Make sure your provider is investing in its infrastructure to ensure your data is handled the right way - day one.

Network Impact

How does the vendor ensure minimal impact on your network, even with high-impact 4k graphics and video content?

WHY SHOULD I CARE?

Many cloud based solutions require a 1:1 connection from media player to cloud server for content downloads and updates. Networks not designed for high bandwidth cloud applications can be crippled when large video updates are deployed to a large mass of media players at once. Intelligent content distribution architecture is critical to ensure minimal impact on your network.

Battle Hardenend

Does the provider work with large brands with specific data-security requirements? How far are they willing to go to ensure compliance with your own data security requirements?

WHY SHOULD I CARE?

Digital signage is a broadcast tool with a huge amount of visibility with your staff and customers. Make sure that the provider you are working with has put forth the effort in testing to ensure that hardware they install on your network is hardened with your security in mind. Ask them to fill out a security questionaire. Make sure you also get an NDA signed between both organizations.

CONTENT

70% of IT and 51% of marketing departments share responsibility for projects. You don't have time to develop code each time someone wants to plug a content source to the screens. That's why it's important to vet out which provider will equip your communications team with the best content feeds and applications.

SUSTAINABLE CONTENT?

1 Successful Programs

Does the provider deliver content programs and applications designed to engage your target audience, keep content up-to-date and minimize the need to use the software?

WHY SHOULD I CARE?

Solid content programs are the key to long term success of your digital signage deployment. A successful content program will combine socially and personally relevant content with core brand content and automatically update with significant frequency. Avoid expensive, digital wallpaper and make sure your provider can put you into content programs as you grow.

2 Measures Success

How often does the vendor walk through your deployment and make recommendations to improve your communications strategy?

WHY SHOULD I CARE?

What you need is access to the experts, not a salesperson. Make sure that your provider helps you set goals for your deployment and checks in on a monthly and quarterly basis to make sure those goals are met. The true pros will have your back to make sure your content continues to inspire the right actions from your audience.

3 Blueprints Your Future

Are you provided with a written, detailed strategy designed to maximize the impact of your communications and minimize your hardware investment?

WHY SHOULD I CARE?

Ask the provider if they provide detailed content plans that address the key needs of your organization. You may have a solid plan already but a well rounded provider will provide you with clarity around all of the boxes that need checked to ensure your plan takes off.

HARDWARE SOFTWARE

SECURITY CONTENT

WWW.INDUSTRYWEAPON.COM

WE ARE YOUR INDUSTRY WEAPON

Industry Weapon is passionate about helping organizations inspire action through communication. When you work with us, you become part of a family dedicated to do everything necessary to ensure success.

Hardware

Industry Weapon boasts **broad media player support** with the largest names in the industry. We understand that many organizations have specific hardware purchasing requirements and have built **solid partnerships with leading hardware manufacturers**.

Digital signage deployments are not one-size-fits-all. Your simple, menuboard today may turn into an interactive kiosk or ultra-high definition video wall tomorrow. **We support the right hardware to best tell your story**

Security

The largest companies in the world trust our infrastructure to deploy their communications on a global scale. Security protocols aren't just a luxury for these brands, they are a must. Industry Weapon's **entire organization is SOC II Audited** and **PCI Compliant**. We take security seriously and will provide INFOSEC teams with all necessary **security documentation** to ease their concerns.

Serving a retail industry and global organizations it neccessary to minimize the impact we have on a clients network. We provide a wide variety of **intelligent data distribution** tools to minimize data consumption in any network configuration scenario..

Software

Our background in UX and web applications drove our focus on **drag-n-drop content creation** from day one. Simple content management and **app-based expandability** allow our users to focus more on the actions they are looking to inspire and less on learning the software.

We learned long ago that everyone says that their software is simple and easy to use. But when the user really needs help, email only support or a clunkly portal doesn't cut it. That's why we led the industry becoming the **first digital signage company to offer Free Training & 24/7 Support**.

Content

Creating content is a headache, even when you have a staff member dedicated solely dedicated to the task. That's why we offer **continuous, free content programs** to our subscribers. These aren't "one size fits all" campaigns, either. We make sure the content is relevant to your signage needs and professionally designed.

With dedicated resources including content strategists at your disposal, our team sets up **quarterly planning sessions** and **detailed content strategy documents** to ensure that your **communications** strategy **inspires action** with your audience.

RISK ASSESSMENT QUESTIONAIRE

HARDWARE

Displays, media players and networking equipment in place to ensure optimal delivery of the digital story.

SOFTWARE

Management, scheduling and distribution are as hands off as possible for the IT Department

SECURITY

Your provider has your best interests in mind, securing your data and ensuring minimal impact on your network.

CONTENT

Your content team is equipped with best of breed content feeds and applications to ensure their success.

Existing vs. New
How can the provider support your existing hardware deployment? Does the provider should offer a robust library of supported devices for a variety of use-cases operating systems and form factors?

Manufacturer Purchasing Preferences
Does the provider offer flexibility to support your preferred hardware manufacturer?

Mixed Deployment Capability
Does the provider support multiple operating systems, with capabilities to manage not just digital signs, but also interactive and video wall situations?

SOC II, PCI, Vulnerability Testing
What level of caution does the provider take to ensure security of your data both in its data centers, code and throughout its day-to-day operations?

Network Impact
How does the vendor ensure minimal impact on your network, even with high-impact 4k graphics and video content?

Battle Hardened
Does the provider work with large brands with specific data-security requirements? How far are they willing to go to ensure compliance with your own data security requirements?

Simplicity
Does the software interface provide similar functionality to the software suites that Marketing & Communications teams are currently using?

Training
Does the provider tie you up in paid training packages or expensive on-site workshops? Or, do they guarantee free, unlimited, one-on-one training is part of your package?

Support
Does your provider offer free, unlimited 24/7 phone and email support? Or are you tied to paid programs to avoid email only, 24-48 hour response times?

Successful Programs
Does the provider deliver content programs and applications designed to engage your target audience, keep content up-to-date and minimize the need to use the software?

Continuous Measurement & Ongoing Planning
How often does the vendor walk through your deployment and make recommendations and provide detailed plans for ongoing success?

Expandable Platform
Does the provider's platform support a variety of third party content applications and services with API's designed to accomodate future expansion?

NOTES

NOTES

NOTES

NOTES

NOTES

NOTES

NOTES

NOTES

NOTES

NOTES